·

SOMETHING TO BELIEVE IN

Something to Believe In

Politics, Professionalism, and Cause Lawyering

STUART A. SCHEINGOLD

and AUSTIN SARAT

Stanford Law and Politics

AN IMPRINT OF STANFORD UNIVERSITY PRESS

STANFORD, CALIFORNIA

2004

Stanford University Press

Stanford, California

www.sup.org

Library of Congress Cataloging-in-Publication Data

Scheingold, Stuart A.
    Something to believe in : politics, professionalism, and cause lawyering /
Stuart A. Scheingold and Austin Sarat.
        p.   cm.
    Includes bibliographical references and index.
    ISBN 0-8047-4947-7 (alk. paper)
        1. Public interest law—United States.   2. Practice of law—Political aspects—United States.   3. Practice of law—United States—Moral and ethical aspects.   I. Sarat, Austin.   II. Title.
KF299.P8S334 2004
340'.023'73—dc22   2004008170

Printed in the United States of America on acid-free, archival-quality paper.

Original Printing 2004

Last figure below indicates year of this printing:
14   13   12   11   10   09   08   07   06   05

Designed and typeset at Stanford University Press in 10 / 14 Palatino.

For Nora, who bore Lee, who sustains me (S.S.)

For Mr. B, my sweet prince (A.S.)

Contents

Acknowledgments

THIS BOOK IS the product of a genuinely collaborative effort which has been ongoing for a decade. For the two of us, it has been a source of extraordinary intellectual stimulation and just plain fun. We have learned a lot and could not imagine doing this same work in any other way. But the collaboration goes well beyond this book's two authors and includes an extraordinary group of scholars who have joined us in the effort to study cause lawyers and helped organize and run conferences, meetings, and panels at professional meetings, where much of our work has been done. Their work has been, or will be, published together in volumes we have edited and provides the basis for much of what we have done in this book. We are grateful to them.

We also are grateful for financial support from the National Science Foundation and Amherst College's Axel Shupf Fund for Intellectual Life. We also wish to acknowledge Scott Barclay, Joel Handler, and Tanina Rostain for their comments on earlier versions of this book and Terrence Halliday who, in many ways, is an unindicted co-conspirator in our work. Thanks also to Mary Ray Worley for her careful and sensitive copyediting, to Amanda Moran, our editor at Stanford University Press, for her help and encouragement as well as to her colleagues at the Press who worked so hard and so professionally to lubricate the wheels of publication.

On the domestic front we have found just the right combination of support and irreverence. We have been offered much constructive advice as well as teased about our passionate interest in an arcane subject called "cause lawyers." For all they do for us, we wish to thank Lee and Stephanie, Lauren, Emily, and Benjamin.

Cause Lawyering and Conventional Lawyering: Professional and Political Perspectives

To do right is noble: to advise others to do right is also noble and much less trouble for yourself.

Mark Twain

AT GATHERINGS of lawyers, talk of alienation and anxiety about their work is frequently present. Worries about increased commercialism, complaints about the costs of their work to family, and stories about the strains of having to provide services to clients whose goals are incompatible with the lawyer's personal moral commitments abound (Kelly, 1994). These worries, complaints, and stories signal what some see as a set of new challenges for lawyers (e.g., Kronman, 1993) and others see as the latest manifestation of a history in which someone seems always to be announcing a "crisis" in the legal profession (Brandeis, 1933; Rhode, 2000b). Whether new or perennial, problems of alienation and signs of anxiety in the profession animate public debate and scholarly concern about lawyers and lawyering (Simon, 1998).

But alienation and anxiety about the nature of lawyering work do not affect all lawyers equally. For those whose idea and practice of lawyering involves service to a cause, many of the symptoms of alienation and anxiety are absent. This is not to suggest that such lawyers have no worries about their work. That is surely not the case. It is to suggest, however, that what William Simon (1998: 1) says about lawyering in general—namely that "no social role encourages such ambitious moral aspirations as the lawyer's, and no social role so consistently disappoints the aspirations it encourages"—is markedly less true of those lawyers whose practices are devoted to the realization of their own moral aspirations.

Moral and political commitment, the defining attributes of cause lawyers are, for most of their peers, relegated to the margins of their professional lives. Conventional or client lawyering involves the deployment of a set of technical skills on behalf of ends determined by the client, not the lawyer (Fried, 1976; Silver and Cross, 2000). Lawyering, in this conception, is neither a domain for moral or political advocacy nor a place to express the lawyer's beliefs about the way society should be organized, disputes resolved, and values expressed.

For cause lawyers, such objectives move from the margins to the center of their professional lives. Lawyering is for them attractive precisely because it is a deeply moral or political activity, a kind of work that encourages pursuit of their vision of the right, the good, or the just. Cause lawyers have *something to believe in* and bring their beliefs to bear in their work lives. In this sense, they are neither alienated from their work nor anxious about the separation of role from person.

This book is devoted to the exploration of the worlds of cause lawyering, of the work that cause lawyers do, of the role of moral and political commitment in their practice, of their relationships to the organized legal profession, and of the contributions they make to democratic politics. We will argue that this kind of lawyering is distinctive in the way it both serves and challenges legal professionalism and in the way it addresses the role of lawyers in democratic society. We will also argue that cause lawyers who wish to maintain their position within the professional project of the organized bar must steer clear of causes which are at odds with mainstream understandings of democracy. Cause lawyers thus emerge as political actors—but as political actors whose work involves doing law. Just as politics animates their legal work, that work disciplines the kinds of politics that they can do. Professional acceptance thus depends on political acquiescence.

On the Definition of Cause Lawyering

Scholarship on cause lawyering is plagued by definitional and conceptual challenges. Indeed it is not possible to provide a single cross-culturally valid definition of cause lawyering. As a result, cause lawyering is a disputed and evolving concept, one that requires researchers to attend to the complex political and professional terrain on which it occurs. At its core, cause lawyering is about using legal skills to pursue ends and ideals that transcend client service—be those ideals social, cultural, political, economic or, indeed, legal (Luban, 1988). Yet cause lawyers are associated with many different causes, function with varying resources and degrees of legitimacy, deploy a wide variety of strategies, and seek extraordinarily diverse goals.

Included under the umbrella of cause lawyering are such polar ideological opposites as poverty and property rights lawyers, feminist and right-to-life lawyers, as well as such disparate pursuits as human rights, environmental, civil liberties, and critical lawyering. Cause lawyering is found in the full range of professional venues: large and small private firms, salaried practice in national and transnational nongovernmental organizations, and government and privately funded lawyering. For better or for worse, this tremendous variation is the hallmark of cause lawyering. Indeed, the term *cause lawyering* conveys a core of meaning which is valid within a wide range of historical and cultural contexts while at the same time being sufficiently inclusive to accommodate a variety of forms.

Definitionally, cause lawyering is associated with both intent and behavior. Serving a cause by accident does not, in our judgment, qualify as cause lawyering. On the other hand, there is evidence that the accidental can be transformed into the intentional when a lawyer's ideals are awakened by service undertaken for other reasons (Barclay and Marshall, forthcoming). Thus, clinical activities in law school, which may be undertaken solely to escape the classroom and gain practical experience, can lead students to cause lawyering because they put students in touch with the problems of marginalized elements of the population. In other words, commitment to a cause can just as easily be a consequence of representation undertaken for different reasons as the other way around (Shamir and Chinsky, 1998). Nor does cause lawyering preclude mixed motives.

Still, whether pure or impure, whether before or after the fact, we deem political or moral commitment an essential and distinguishing feature of cause lawyering. Lawyers are drawn to causes by a search for something in which to believe or as an outlet to express their already formed beliefs. Although cause lawyering is in general a low status and poorly paid professional activity, it does provide what conventional legal ethics deny—the opportunity to harmonize personal conviction and professional life.

One of the most noteworthy things that has emerged from the recent spate of research on cause lawyering in the United States and elsewhere is just how widespread cause lawyering has become (see Sarat and Scheingold, 1998a, 2001a). In the United States, the principal focus of this book, cause lawyering has flourished at least since the 1960s. This has been due in large part to the successes of the civil rights movement and to the work of a number of well-established social advocacy organizations like the NAACP Legal Defense Fund, the Environmental Defense Fund, the Center for Constitutional Rights, and many others. The emergence of cause lawyering elsewhere in the world can be traced to a combination of factors, including the spread of written constitutions and constitutional courts, the neoliberal values driving globalization, and the development of transnational human rights networks (Sarat and Scheingold, 2001b).

It is thus important to appreciate at the outset just how protean and heterogeneous an enterprise cause lawyering is—an enterprise which grows and reinvents itself in confrontations with a vast array of challenges. Nonetheless, there are recurrent themes and patterns that enable us to bring some order to this apparent chaos—while at the same time illuminating the loci of cause lawyering within the legal profession.

Both the variations within cause lawyering and its underlying unity emerge as one considers its goals and strategies. In terms of goals, cause lawyers array themselves along a left-right political continuum. With respect to strategy, the choice tends to be more dichotomous—that is between legal and political strategies. While each of these elements of cause lawyering will be treated separately, we see them as interdependent and will indicate how and why this is the case.

What we call cause lawyering is often referred to as public interest lawyering within the legal profession and among academics. However, we prefer *cause lawyering* because it is an inclusive term. It conveys a determination to take sides in political and moral struggle without making distinctions between worthy and unworthy causes. Conversely, to talk about public interest lawyering is to take on irresolvable disputes about what is, or is not, in the public interest. Whether the pursuit of any particular cause advances the public interest is very much in the eye of the beholder.

Invocations of the public interest have a long history in the literature of reform (Lasswell, 1962: 54). Muckrakers from time immemorial have railed against the special interests in the name of the public and its interest (Niemeyer, 1962: 1). But what is the public interest and how is it defined?

The public interest is a notoriously slippery concept, which generally does little or no analytic work. According to one scholar (Schubert, 1960: 33, quoting E. E. Schattschneider), "The public interest may be described as the aggregate of common interests, including the common interest in seeing that there is fair play among private interests. The public interest is not the mere sum of the special interests, and it is certainly not the sum of the organized special interests. Nor is it an automatic consequence of the struggle of the special interests." In this conception, discovering the public interest is a "value neutral technical process" (Schubert, 1960: 31). Recently Deborah Rhode (2000b: 17) has argued that all lawyering should be animated by the public interest and that "lawyers' conduct needs consistent, disinterested, and generalizable foundations."

Unfortunately, as David Truman (1951: 51) long ago observed, such appeals "do not describe any actual or possible political situation within a complex modern nation. . . . We do not need to account for a totally inclusive interest, because one does not exist." The public interest neither identifies any interest, nor can it point the way toward policy or reform. Instead, the "primary function of the concept in our language is to convey approval or commendation." (Flathman, 1966: 4). It "serves as a symbol to legitimize the acts of any group that can successfully identify itself with it in the public mind" (Long, 1952: 809). For cause lawyers, the way to justice is the way of politics, a way that names and defends interests with particularity and acknowledges the conflicts and costs which the pursuit of those interests necessarily entails. This assertive engagement in the contentious issues of public life is one way in which lawyering provides something to believe in.

Our objective in this introductory chapter is to clarify the nature of cause lawyering through an exploration of the ethical ideals driving conventional and cause lawyering respectively, of the various roles that cause lawyers play in advancing different conceptions of democracy, and of the strategic choices that cause lawyers necessarily face. We choose these starting points because both cause lawyers and conventional practitioners see themselves as divided by, and united in, a professional project which provides a public good. This ethical discourse over the nature of legal professionalism and its contribution to society is captured in the contrasting answers of conventional and cause lawyers to one deceptively simple ethical question. Should lawyering be driven primarily by client service, or are lawyers entitled, even obligated, to serve objectives that transcend service to clients?

Cause lawyers identify explicitly, and without apologies, with the latter possibility. In so doing, they distinguish themselves from, and put themselves ethically at odds with, the vast majority of lawyers, who see their primary professional responsibility as providing high-quality service to individuals and organizations without being substantively committed to the ends of those clients. Of course, cause lawyers also serve their clients but tend to see client service as a means to their moral and political ends. Accordingly, conventional practitioners are likely to view cause lawyering as ethically suspect at best (Bell, 1976). In sharp contrast, cause lawyers believe that they are responding to higher ethical standards. Cause lawyering thus stands in an ambiguous relationship to the professional project of the organized bar.

To the extent that there is room for cause lawyering within that project the place of cause lawyering depends on its possible contributions to liberal democracy and on the strategic choices cause lawyers make. As advocates for liberal-legal rights, cause lawyers occupy a shared terrain with other lawyers whether or not they are motivated by commitment to a cause or service to a client. As they stretch the boundaries of liberal-legalism and advocate in a more politicized way, they transgress even the most capacious understandings of conventional legal professionalism.

Cause Lawyers and the Legal Profession

It is important to acknowledge that both cause and conventional lawyers have ideals, that conventional lawyers are not simply cynical maximizers of their own wealth and status, and that cause lawyers are not simply altruistic and self-abnegating (for an example of this position, see Menkel-Meadow, 1992; 1998). However, the ideals of conventional and cause lawyering are dramatically different. According to the ethical codes of the legal profession here and in some other countries, it is the essential duty of lawyers to provide vigorous and skillful representation. Irrespective of whether lawyers approve of a client's moral stance, they are supposed to provide zealous advocacy on the client's behalf.

Conventional lawyers are not, therefore, supposed to have any qualms about switching sides or representing clients whose values and behavior are reprehensible to them. The prevailing codes of professional ethics expressly allow lawyers to represent clients without endorsing their views or goals. The rules allow the sale of legal expertise without requiring a lawyer to take into account any of the moral or political implications of their representation.[1] Indeed, to do so is a point of professional pride and a demonstration of professional responsibility. British barristers are, thus, readily prepared to both prosecute and defend in criminal cases—in accordance with the "cab-rank" rule. Similarly, the noted American "litigator" David Boies probably considers it a hallmark of his professionalism to have successfully represented IBM in an antitrust suit brought by the U.S. Justice Department and subsequently to have represented the Justice Department in an antitrust suit brought against Microsoft. More broadly, politically liberal U.S. lawyers, including Boies, think nothing of working on behalf of corporations, on the one hand, and serving liberal causes or serving in Democratic administrations on the other. Conventional practitioners would see anyone who characterizes this flexibility as inconsistent or cynical as confusing professional ethics with personal morality.

The rationale for this bedrock of professionalism is simple, straightforward, and readily embraced by other professions—as, for example, by doctors and by such would-be professionals as police officers. Professionalism is, in this framing, measured largely in terms of technical expertise put at the disposal of clients, patients, or the public (in the case of police officers). William Simon (1978), writing specifically and critically about lawyers, refers to this ethical code as the "ideology of advocacy"—according to which attorneys are supposed to be professionally partisan but personally neutral advocates for their clients. Client interests are to be defended zealously but the attorney is to maintain neutrality with respect to any broader social, political, or economic interests that may be at stake in the conflict between the parties to the litigation. In this view, detachment and distance, which might be viewed as sources and symptoms of alienation, are deemed essential to a reasoned defense of the client's immediate interests.

Conversely, to identify closely with the aspirations of clients is believed likely to compromise effective representation by engaging the attorney's morality and emotions and endangering her or his rationality. As we will see in Chapter 3, a determination to privilege rationality and purge morality and emotion from lawyering figures prominently in legal education. It is, in effect, a quintessential rite-of-passage for turning talented laity into competent lawyers. Conversely, moral and emotional engagement—whether pro or con—is said to work at cross-purposes to service excellence.

Cause lawyers reject this way of thinking about the professional project—choosing to privilege their moral aspirations and political purposes even if doing so leads to violations of the profession's ethical code (Sarat, 1998a). They expressly seek clients with whom they agree and causes in which they believe (Simon, 1984). Not only are they eager to take sides in social conflict and to identify themselves with the sides they take, but they are determined to construct their legal practice around this taking of sides. They deny that their effectiveness will be put at risk by the values they share with their clients. Indeed, cause lawyers often argue that the more closely they identify with their clients' values, the better advocates they will be (Sterett, 1998). Shared values, according to this perspective, are conducive to a deeper understanding that will enable them to engage in context-sensitive advocacy.

Cause lawyers tend to transform the nature of legal advocacy—becoming advocates not only, or primarily, for their clients but for causes and, one might say, for their own beliefs. In thus reversing the priorities of the organized legal profession and in staking out the moral high ground, cause lawyers challenge their professional community.

Convergence Between Conventional and Cause Lawyering

At first glance, it might therefore seem that cause and conventional lawyers inhabit entirely different and mutually antagonistic professional worlds. Yet there are points of convergence and overlap that blur the widely acknowledged distinctions between them. Many so-called conventional lawyers tend to represent primarily, perhaps exclusively, those with whom they agree (Rosen, 2001). This certainly seems to be the case with many, perhaps most, lawyers who represent corporations. Consider also personal injury lawyers in the United States. They are divided between a plaintiffs' bar and a defense bar. The plaintiffs' bar represents almost exclusively individuals or classes of individuals who have been injured—whether as consumers, workers, victims of police abuse, or the like. Conversely, the defense bar represents only the targets of such suits—typically business corporations and insurance companies. Thus, these and many other conventional practitioners certainly fail to convey the requisite sense of neutrality called for by the ideology of advocacy. However, many of these conventional practitioners would deny what cause lawyers proudly proclaim—that they are self-consciously choosing sides in basic social conflicts (Kagan and Rosen, 1985).[2]

Consider also that many cause lawyers use conventional legal practices to finance low-fee or no-fee representation of causes in which they believe (Shamir and Chinsky, 1998). Similarly, lawyers in conventional corporate practice frequently set aside a portion of their time to provide pro bono advocacy for a variety of causes to which they are committed (Rhode, 2000b). All of this will be considered when we explore the sites of cause lawyering practice in Chapter 4. Suffice it to say, for the time being, that although cause and conventional lawyers are marching to distinctly different ethical drummers, there is often substantial convergence and overlap in the ways that they practice law.

Some scholars have advocated reforms in the legal profession's ethical codes which, if implemented, would further close the gap between conventional and cause lawyers. Thus Deborah Rhode (2000b: 211) argues that "the greatest source of discontent among today's lawyers is their perceived lack of contribution to social justice." As a response she suggests that all lawyers "need to assume greater moral responsibility for the consequences of their professional conduct." Similarly William Simon (1998: 9), again writing about all lawyers, suggests that the basic maxim for a reformed code of professional ethics is that "the lawyer should take such actions as, considering the relevant circumstances of the particular case, seem likely to promote justice."

In addition, there is a long-standing tradition, going back at least to de Tocqueville (1876), of viewing conventional legal practice as a bulwark of civil society and liberal democracy. Accordingly, the profession has regularly represented itself as providing a public good—in return, some have argued, for an official entitlement to monopolize the provision of legal services (Abel, 1981). To our way of thinking, it is not important whether this broader vision of professional responsibility is attributable to a strategic quid pro quo or to taking seriously the conception of the legal profession as a foundational social institution. Either way, conventional lawyers in general and the organized profession in particular clearly take comfort from a belief that the whole of their enterprise of client representation is somehow bigger and more beneficent than the sum of its parts.

This widely proclaimed conception of lawyering as a higher calling leads to convergence between some types of conventional practice and cause lawyering (Silver and Cross, 2000). The result is, on the one hand, to add to the complexity of disentangling cause and conventional lawyering. Nonetheless, we will argue that there is a meaningful distinction—albeit with some contestable conceptual terrain at the point of convergence. To think of law as a higher calling leads almost inevitably to some receptivity to cause lawyering among conventional practitioners. We will argue that the extent of convergence and receptivity depends not only on the way in which cause lawyering is practiced—an issue to be pursued in the next section. In addition, we see receptivity as directly related to how conventional lawyers interpret their own higher calling.

The Lawyer as Peacemaker

In its narrowest framing, the notion of legal practice as a public good means that partisan, neutral, and skilled client representation, as such, should enhance the quality and character of civil society. One of the most prominent and outspoken advocates of this position is Mary Ann Glendon (1994). She begins with de Tocqueville's observations about law and lawyers as the balance wheel of American democracy. She goes on to decry what she sees as the decline of professional ethics, which has undermined the once inextricable connections among the practice of law, civility in society, and American democracy. At the heart of the problem, as she sees it (1994: 5), are prototypical cause lawyers with the "hubris" to see themselves as "vindicators of an ever-expanding array of claims and rights." Instead, she wishes to see a return to the kinds of "client representation and public service" that she characterizes as the "golden age" of the legal profession—an era she believes ended in the 1960s (1994: 13).[3]

Note that Glendon couples client representation with public service while identifying the pursuit of expanded civil rights with personal hubris. In this equation she makes clear her hostility to cause lawyering. Coming from a conservative like Glendon, this argument could be easily dismissed as no more than a political polemic. Glendon is, however, building from a well-established intellectual and professional understanding of the contribution that lawyers as wise counselors can make in lubricating the wheels of business, society, and politics.

This vision of legal practice as public service per se is altogether consistent with Talcott Parsons's functional school of legal sociology. According to Parsons (1962: 58), law and lawyers contribute distinctively and significantly to social integration. "Let us suggest that in the larger social perspective the primary function of a legal system is integrative. It serves to mitigate potential elements of conflict and to oil the machinery of social intercourse."[4]

Lawyers enhance the law's integrative role by contributing to "mechanisms for the 'cooling off' of the passions aroused" by social conflict (Parsons, 1962: 68). They do so, in the first place, by simultaneously representing the client and the law. Their influence, according to Parsons, stems from bringing the client's case in a nonjudgmental way to the authoritative institutions of the society.

Conversely, the lawyer conveys to the client the authority of the law and the legitimacy of its decision-making process.[5]

As Glendon (1994: chapter 3) sees it, in her so-called golden age, litigation was a last resort. These days, in contrast, aggressive litigation is privileged, as is the uncompromising pursuit of rights by lawyers who are increasingly "connoisseurs of conflict." Glendon's (1994: 278) vision is, then, of the "lawyer as peacemaker and problem solver." She deems this now neglected and rejected professional ideal a particularly painful loss at a time when our society is fragmented, diverse, and desperately in need of reintegration.[6] In any event, Glendon's particular vision of private practice as public service is especially inimical to the aggressive pursuit of rights associated with cause lawyering.

The Lawyer-Statesman

There are, however, broader visions of conventional lawyering as a public good that, though more consonant with cause lawyering, remain distinct from it. Anthony Kronman (1993) expresses this broader vision by linking conventional lawyering to "public-spirited" idealism. As he defines the term, a public-spirited lawyer acts on behalf of the long-term "integrity or well-being of the legal system as a whole" (1993: 118). With this vocabulary, Kronman seeks to make all lawyers public interest lawyers.

While Kronman (1993: 118) acknowledges that it is judges rather than practicing lawyers who have the primary responsibility for nurturing public-spiritedness within the legal profession, he argues on both "idealistic" and "realistic" grounds for a vision of legal practice that incorporates "deliberative wisdom and civic-mindedness" into counseling clients and advocacy on their behalf (1993: 122–23). Kronman's case for this broader vision of legal practice is, however, firmly tethered to serving client interests. In his view, the client's true interests are served by preserving the integrity of the legal system, and an accomplished attorney has the wisdom, the experience, and the credibility to broaden the client's vision. Moreover, because counseling and advocacy take place, whether directly or indirectly, under the aegis of courts, attorneys can and should call attention to public-spirited ideals that drive judges. In short, Kronman's public spirit is really ancillary to, and defined by, client service—albeit an enlightened view thereof.

Kronman (1993: 12) does, however, identify a more wholehearted commitment to public-spiritedness among "lawyer-statesmen." What is a lawyer-statesman? Kronman applies the term principally to lawyers who engage in public service—most often by taking time out from their legal practices with prestigious Wall Street firms. Among twentieth-century exemplars to whom Kronman points are former cabinet members, Henry Stimson, Dean Acheson, and Cyrus Vance, as well such influential presidential advisers as John McCloy, who administered the postwar occupation of Germany, and disarmament negotiator Paul Warnke. Kronman traces this tradition to nineteenth-century figures like John Marshall and Daniel Webster.

Kronman (1993: 12) claims that lawyers are uniquely "possessed of great practical wisdom and exceptional persuasive powers, devoted to the public good but keenly aware of the limitations of human beings and their political arrangements." Tocqueville (1876: 351) offers a similar but more ambivalent assessment of the values that lawyers, as lawyers, bring to politics. "Lawyers are attached to public order beyond every other consideration, and the best security of public order is authority. It must not be forgotten, also, that if they prize freedom much, they generally value legality still more: they are less afraid of tyranny than of arbitrary power; and provided the legislature undertakes of itself to deprive men of their independence, they are not dissatisfied." But irrespective of how it is inflected, this coupling of prudence, the well-being of the legal system, and the well-being of the Republic does offer a professional ideal that explicitly links law and lawyers to the polity.

In the final analysis, however, the lawyer-statesman fails to provide professional sustenance for cause lawyering. After all, the lawyer-statesman vision of ethical responsibility is, at best, only conditionally applicable to legal practice—where it tends to be trumped by client service. Put another way, even as conceived by Kronman, lawyers can best serve public purposes outside of legal practice—as judges or as part-time government officials. In addition, there is the association of the lawyer-statesman with elite lawyers from the best law schools whose professional lives are bound up with large law firms serving corporate clients. At the very least, it would seem that lawyers so closely identified with the powerful might be unreliable agents of the many causes that run counter to the interests of those at the top.

While neither Glendon's nor Kronman's ideal lawyers are cause lawyers, their quests to validate lawyering as a public good open the door to ethical visions that are consonant with, or supportive of, cause lawyering. Still, as we will argue in the next section, the ethical convergence of cause and conventional lawyering is very restricted. The result is that cause lawyering remains in an ambiguous and contested position within the legal profession.

Advancing the Goals of Liberal Legalism Within a Democratic Polity

Only when the ethical responsibilities of lawyers are defined in terms of justice and are imposed directly on legal practice do they cross over into the terrain of cause lawyering. Crossing that boundary does not necessarily cut off cause lawyers from the support of conventional lawyers. However, only narrowly legal conceptions of justice are incorporated into conventionally accepted understandings of a lawyer's ethical responsibilities. Conversely, efforts to define justice in political, social, and economic terms are regarded with considerable suspicion by the organized legal profession (Simon, 1984).

To begin with, the ethical ideal of providing representation for those who could not otherwise afford it is entirely uncontroversial. Of course, individual lawyers may not view this as an ethical responsibility of their own. Similarly, they may look with some condescension on those who devote their career to such representation——as, for example, public defenders or staff lawyers in legal services programs. This work is likely to be viewed as unchallenging, because advanced legal skills are neither tested nor rewarded—or so it seems to conventional practitioners in general and elite lawyers in particular.

Nonetheless, most conventional practitioners, and certainly those speaking for the profession as a whole, recognize that such work does help to keep the scales of justice in balance (Luban, 1984). In addition, there is general recognition that providing access to justice for those who could not otherwise afford it can embellish the reputation of the legal profession (Rhode, 2000b). In short, serving the poor tends to be widely acclaimed as doing good, even if the lawyers who do so are looked down upon for not doing well. Note, for example, that corporate lawyers who donate their service pro bono can have it both ways. They are recognized as part of the professional elite and praised for their devotion to equal justice under law.

Lawyering on behalf of recognized constitutional rights occupies much the same ethical high ground. Bill of Rights lawyering can generate controversy—particularly insofar as it entails efforts to extend the reach of recognized rights. In other words, the aggressive pursuit of a Bill of Rights agenda—the work of the American Civil Liberties Union is prototypical—is both an honored and, at the same time, a suspect element of lawyering for justice. The controversy that frequently accompanies such activities can certainly make the organized legal profession uncomfortable. On the other hand, since this work often involves appellate litigation, Bill of Rights lawyering tends to carry substantial prestige. Here, as with access to justice lawyering, there are few ethical or professional minefields to be negotiated by Bill of Rights lawyers.

There are, however, many such minefields lying just beyond Bill of Rights lawyering—once, that is, cause lawyers turn their attention from legal justice, defined by rights enshrined in the Constitution, to social, economic, and political advocacy. Once justice is defined in these broader terms—what David Luban (1988: 160) describes as moral activism—ethical waters and professional standing become increasingly murky and precarious. The major objection noted by Luban focuses on the extent to which the nature of representation is transformed when lawyers commit themselves to righting social, economic, and political wrongs. It is at this point that the classic tension between cause and client emerges. "I will call it the 'double agent problem,'" Luban (1988: 319) writes, "because it originates in the fact that the lawyer is an agent for both the client and the cause; as the name suggests, the role of double agent carries within it the seeds of betrayal."[7]

Luban's (1988) analysis thus moves the locus of ethical discourse squarely into the realm of cause lawyering. However, it also reveals that there is an intrinsic and pervasive ethical tension between cause and conventional lawyering, which means that cause lawyering is, almost by definition, a suspect enterprise. Yet, as we have argued, because the legal profession has long proclaimed that lawyering is a public good, which transcends client representation as such, there is some space for cause lawyering within mainstream professional discourse. But that professional welcome is decidedly conditional—depending on how cause lawyering is practiced.

Cause Lawyering and Democratic Possibilities

One of the constants in cause lawyering is its identification with democracy—and, in particular, liberal forms of democracy. In this regard, cause lawyering tends to replicate the record of the legal profession in general while, at the same time, reinforcing the broader liberal-legal homology (Halliday and Karpik, 1997). However, there are competing democratic narratives among cause lawyers. Three of these narratives are liberal democratic: left-liberal, neoliberal, and libertarian. In addition, there also three narratives which challenge liberal democracy: social democratic and emancipatory democratic on the left and evangelical democratic on the right. When we analyze democratic advocacy in Chapter 5, these narratives will be specified in some detail, as will be the distinctive forms of cause lawyering associated with each of them. Some preliminary points are, however, appropriate for this introductory chapter.

Note that there are among cause lawyers divisions between left and right and between opponents and defenders of liberal democracy. We will demonstrate in Chapter 5 why the latter distinction is more salient to an understanding of the opportunities for, and the obstacles to, cause lawyering. Suffice it to say for the time being that working within the liberal democratic paradigm provides cause lawyers with both professional and political legitimacy, as well as with ready access to the constitutional processes that are at the core of cause lawyering. Conversely, insofar as cause lawyers pursue transformative agendas, they must do so with fewer political and legal resources and with poorer professional prospects. These generalizations apply to friends and to opponents of liberal democracy on both the left and right.

Democracy broadly conceived thus represents a defining point of both convergence and contention among cause lawyers. We stake out different democratic narratives not because we believe cause lawyers can be readily compartmentalized but, instead, because of what these narratives reveal about the nature of cause lawyering. Individual cause lawyers may well in the course of their careers cross and recross the boundaries dividing democratic narratives from one another—driven, for example, by changes in the political context, conditions at the practice site, or personal circumstances (Scheingold, 1998). Taken together, however, these diverse democratic narratives do bear witness to inextricable connections for cause lawyers among career prospects, professional status, available resources, strategies pursued, and likelihood of achieving objectives. Cause lawyers experience the pull of the profession as a disciplining and domesticating force, policing the kinds of causes for which lawyers can and should advocate and the nature of the advocacy they provide.

Strategic Choice: Litigation Versus Politicization

The major strategic question confronting cause lawyers in the United States is whether to engage legally or politically. Legal engagement, what might be termed rule-of-law cause lawyering, means giving priority to the courts and litigation—whether through class actions, amicus briefs, or by raising legal and constitutional issues in connection with the representation of particular clients. Conversely, political cause lawyering functions in multiple venues ranging from lobbying through political mobilization and organization to street demonstrations and civil disobedience (McCann and Silverstein, 1998)—even the way law offices themselves are organized (Trubek and Kransberger, 1998). Political cause lawyering also can involve participation in social movements—both as movement activists and as attorneys supporting direct political action. What lawyers do in these several venues may be coordinated with one another or go forward separately. Thus, political strategies, while not precluding litigation, are more likely to entail lobbying, direct action (or support of direct action), and so forth.

To engage politically entails overt identification with, and commitment to, the political agenda of one side in conflicts over constitutional rights, welfare and environmental policies, electoral arrangements, and the like. In pursuing a political path, cause lawyers, in effect, declare their solidarity with their clients and the causes they jointly pursue. Solidarity is a marker of political cause lawyering, in part, because cause lawyers who thus become enmeshed with their clients' agendas do so in order to make a political statement and are ordinarily perceived as doing so by outsiders. For them law is merely a tool in political struggle. Yet politically engaged cause lawyers may not see political and legal strategies as mutually exclusive. Nonetheless, the logic and the trajectory of solidaristic representation leads inevitably to privileging cause over legal and ethical constraints (Sarat, 1998a). Conversely, rule-of-law cause lawyers tend to identify with rights, legality, and constitutionality as ends in themselves. For the politically engaged cause lawyer, both the client and the law are treated as means rather than ends. For the legally engaged cause lawyer, legality is, in effect, the cause.[8]

Conclusion

This chapter has presented two arguments. The first is that cause lawyering is most readily compatible with the means and ends of liberal democracy and that liberal democratic cause lawyering challenges, but also legitimates, legal professionalism. The second argument points to the multiplicity of forms that cause lawyering takes and, more specifically, the consequences of these different forms for democracy and professionalism. In the course of this book we will explore both of these arguments.

Cause lawyers in liberal democratic states can take advantage of a liberal-legal homology rooted in state structures, the culture of the legal profession, and the interaction between them. This means that cause lawyering on behalf of liberal democratic values in a liberal democratic state functions within, rather than in opposition to, mainstream visions of lawyer professionalism.[9] Conversely, to struggle against this liberal-legal homology on behalf of a transformative agenda has substantial political and professional drawbacks.

Insofar as cause lawyering opposes prevailing state forms, it faces especially formidable obstacles. It is one thing to ask the state to live up to its own ideals and quite another to pursue transformation of those ideals. Generally speaking, then, the further cause lawyers move from the liberal democratic center, the more precarious become their political, as well as their professional, prospects. Those cause lawyers who are committed to fundamental political transformation are often forced into more confrontational strategies. At the same time, they are, implicitly and contradictorily, dependent on the state that they wish to transform. Alan Thomson (1992: 6) describes this contradiction as an effort to deploy "the law to fight the system which (theory tells us) law maintains."

Insofar as transformative objectives lead cause lawyers beyond rule-of-law strategies to political and even extralegal tactics, they move outside of the profession's definition of acceptable conduct and thus court professional opprobrium. Generally speaking, to engage legally means functioning at least partially, if ambivalently, within the boundaries of mainstream professionalism (Sarat and Scheingold, 1998b: 3–4). This terrain may well be controversial and can even become a minefield for those who are deemed to be representing a socially constructed "other" in too aggressive a way. On the whole, however, legally engaged cause lawyering may actually embellish an attorney's professional reputation (Sarat and Scheingold, 1998a).

In contrast, to politicize one's legal practice is to test and probably to violate the nethermost boundaries of mainstream professionalism, and this ordinarily means incurring substantial career costs. Moreover, insofar as the public associates cause lawyering with radical or subversive causes, cause lawyers are, in effect, putting the profession's social capital at risk. It is thus one thing for cause lawyers to vindicate widely accepted rights and quite another to become advocates in political struggles that challenge the state or the deeply rooted values from which its legitimacy is derived.

The relationship between cause lawyering and liberal democracy will be pursued in more detail in the chapters that follow. Along the way, we will continue to insist on the complex relations of cause lawyering, professionalism, and politics. As we examine cause lawyering we will attend especially to its embeddedness in various institutional frameworks composed of the organized bar, law schools, practice settings, and the legal and political agencies of American democracy. Each provides opportunities for cause lawyers; each imposes constraints on them.

In the chapters that follow we take up these institutional contexts, examining how they both nurture and limit cause lawyering. In addition, we take up the variability of the phenomenon and the sources of this variation. Among these sources of variation are the multiple goals that constitute the universe of cause lawyering, the different mixes of constraints and incentives that are to be found at the many sites of cause lawyering practice, and changes in the professional and political climates in which cause lawyers practice. In addition, we will analyze the consequences of these different forms of practice in order to explain what cause lawyers can hope to accomplish, how they can best do so, as well as the status and career implications of different kinds of cause lawyering practice.

To this end, the next chapter will look in greater detail at the history of the relationship between cause lawyering and the organized legal profession. Chapter 3 will look at the role of legal education in developing the kind of moral and political advocacy that characterizes cause lawyering. Chapter 4 will turn to the practice of cause lawyering in its many sites—public and private, salaried and fee-for-service, and so on. In Chapter 5, we return to the roles of cause lawyering in democracy and the consequences of those roles for the standing of cause lawyers in the legal profession. Finally, Chapter 6 looks forward, considering the ways new democratic possibilities and pressures in a globalizing world may alter the terrain of cause lawyering.

Cause Lawyering, Civic Professionalism, and the Organized Legal Profession: A Brief History

WHILE CAUSE lawyering may help alleviate problems of alienation and anxiety about work that plague the contemporary legal profession, it complicates the meaning of lawyer professionalism and challenges conventional understandings of the appropriate relationship between professionalism and politics. The legal profession both needs and, at the same time, is threatened by cause lawyering. It seeks both to make room for and to rein in lawyers' political and moral commitments.

On the one hand, cause lawyering is rooted in traditions of civic responsibility that long have been intrinsic to the ethical ideals of lawyering in the United States. Cause lawyers serve the interests of the profession by reconnecting law and morality and by making tangible the idea that lawyering is a "public profession"—one whose contribution to society goes beyond the acquisition, aggregation, and deployment of technical skills (see Brandeis, 1933; and Gordon, 1984, 1986). Yet cause lawyering exposes the limitations of the dominant conception of professionalism. It stretches the meaning of civic professionalism well beyond the Tocquevillian vision of social responsibility and engagement while at the same time directly assailing the profession's core standard of ethical behavior, which weds lawyering to political and moral neutrality and to technical competence.

In challenging the adequacy of professional responsibility as client service and introducing, for example, the political question of whose interests are served by the conventional vision of "neutral but partisan" legal representation (Abel, 1981), cause lawyering reveals the dominant conception of professionalism as contingent and constructed. Moreover, in offering a politicized alternative, cause lawyering destabilizes the ongoing professional project and puts at risk the political immunity of the legal profession. Thus, to understand the ethical tensions discussed in Chapter 1 is to take an important initial step toward explaining the profession's ambivalence to cause lawyering as well as to open up the question of under what conditions the organized legal profession is willing, however warily, to accept cause lawyering.

To answer that question, it is necessary to look beyond ethical arguments to history, to the efforts of the organized legal profession to protect and enhance its own social capital as well as the prosperity of American lawyers. More specifically, we must look to the organized profession's obligations undertaken as part of the bargain it struck with the state in return for the right to monopolize the delivery of legal services. We are particularly interested in the activities of the *organized* legal profession, because it was only after lawyers had established a collective social and political presence that they were able to act in concert to articulate a shared understanding of lawyer professionalism. For the organized bar, legitimation of lawyering as a bulwark of civil society has been a key objective. In this chapter we suggest that when the reputation of the profession has been under attack, the legitimacy it derives from cause lawyering can sometimes provide much-needed political leverage.

During the period at the end of the nineteenth and the beginning of the twentieth centuries when the profession was organizing under the aegis of the American Bar Association (ABA), it was driven by values and interests that were inimical to cause lawyering. Slowly and unevenly over the course of the last century the organized legal profession came to terms with cause lawyers so that by the 1960s a cautious alliance between the bar and cause lawyering seemed to be emerging. Since then there has been as much caution as alliance in this relationship.

The boundaries of the mainstream legal profession's accommodation to cause lawyering are defined by a convergence between the profession's objectives in the marketplace and the polity, on the one hand, and by its increasing support for equal justice and constitutional rights on the other. Because, as we will argue, the reputations of lawyers in general and the ABA in particular were seriously sullied by their roles in some of most noteworthy and regrettable events of the 1960s and early 1970s, an association with cause lawyering became strategically valuable. It is, however, also important to add that during these years the ranks of the ABA came increasingly to include attorneys who were responsive to the rights consciousness that characterized the era.[1]

The place of cause lawyering in the profession remains both conditional and precarious. Certainly there has been at best a grudging recognition of moral and political advocacy. However, we will demonstrate that even conditional receptivity by the organized bar provides cause lawyers with some political leverage and career opportunities—albeit at the margins of the basic professional project.

The Elements of Professionalism

In its effort to identify common ground among lawyers and to lend coherence to their practices, the organized bar has historically invested in the ideology of professionalism. Yet it treats professionalism not as an ideology, but as a thing with a set of essential attributes (Gabel, 1982). These attributes are supposed to distinguish occupations from professions and professions from one another. Only insofar as lawyers share among themselves agreed-upon standards of technical competence and ethical probity are they entitled to monopolize the provision of legal services. Professionalism provides the basis for these claims of competence and probity and, in this way, lays the groundwork for the privileges that are accorded to lawyers (Abbott, 1988).

The experienced world of legal professionalism is, however, much more complex than the organized profession would have us believe (see Nelson and Trubek, 1992a). Two claims are at the core of professionalism's privileged status—namely that professionals are both uniquely knowledgeable and resolutely trustworthy. This combination of expertise and integrity constitutes the profession's guarantee to the public of service excellence (Goode, 1957; Friedson, 1972). To claim status as a professional is, in other words, to assert both competence and responsibility. Insofar, then, as lawyers are seen as professionals, they are recognized as agents of justice—in much the same way as doctors are agents of health. This recognition entitles lawyers, doctors, and other certified professionals to control access to their professions and to discipline members who disregard their professional responsibilities. In short, it is as recognized professionals that individual practitioners and their associations gain an institutionalized status as participants in civil society (Johnson, 1972).

From this perspective, it is the primary role of professional organizations like the American Bar Association and the American Medical Association to function as guardians of quality control. On the one hand, they become intimately involved with professional education—ordinarily through establishing accreditation standards for the institutions that train their practitioners. On the other hand, they establish and administer disciplinary mechanisms to deal with ethical transgressions. In so doing, they seek to assure the public that it is being protected from quacks and charlatans.

Professionalism as Constructed and Contested

It is probably fair to say that the public more readily acknowledges the legal profession's expertise than its integrity. In part, this is because the public finds it difficult to understand, much less to take comfort in, zealous advocacy as the bedrock of professional responsibilities (Rhode, 2000b). The so-called ideology of advocacy (Simon, 1978) is difficult to reconcile with a vision of lawyers as agents of justice. Another source of distrust stems from the ABA's role as a trade association dedicated to protecting the income of its members. As Terence Halliday and Lucien Karpik (1997: 3) put it, drawing on Magali Sarfatti Larson's analysis in *The Rise of Professionalism* (1977): "What were construed by professionals as noble features of self-regulation turned out, on inspection, to be ideologically camouflaged pretenses for artificially created scarcity of supply of services, for boosting prices of services, and for thereby excluding large numbers of potential consumers from the market for professional services."[2]

Scholarly critics share the public's skepticism. They describe professionalism as constructed rather than as defined by a set of essential attributes. For them it is a way of describing the concepts and institutions through which occupations seek control of the market for their services (see, e.g., Larson, 1977; Johnson, 1972). Moreover, while the bar emphasizes the underlying unity of lawyers, critics highlight stratification (see Abel, 1987; Hagan, Huxter, and Parker 1988) and conflict (Bucher and Strauss, 1961). They argue that professionalism is a tool used by particular segments of the bar to assert and protect their own privileged positions against the challenges of outside groups (Auerbach, 1976). Professionalism is, in this view, an excuse for excluding those groups and for marginalizing new entrants to the bar. Instead of building consensus, enhancing ethical standards, and raising levels of competence, professionalism is seen by these critics as a top-down project of social control (Abel, 1981). In sum, there are those who would argue that market control *is* the professional project (Abel, 1981).

But professionalism should not be seen merely as a rhetorical device which disguises the pursuit of self-interest as public-spiritedness (see Friedson, 1972; Auerbach, 1976; Illich, 1977). It can also be thought of as providing a linguistic passageway from the expression of particular preferences and interests to the taken-for-granted realm of seemingly eternal verities and uncontested, essential truths. Use of that passageway is particularly salient in periods when lawyers' practices are, or are perceived to be, unsettled. Especially at those times, there is as much division as unity and as much conflict as consensus over the meaning of professionalism (Solomon, 1992). Professionalism becomes, under those circumstances, a means through which lawyers respond to changes in their community and their practices. It is, moreover, a way of marking differences, of translating those differences into issues of right and wrong and of staking out a claim to the high moral ground.

As ideology, professionalism takes on meaning in the localities and conditions in which lawyers practice. Place and time shape the fragments and configurations used to construct a variety of maps of social reality, each claiming the label of professionalism (Nelson and Trubek, 1992a). This elasticity makes professionalism available as symbolic capital in the clash of cultures among lawyers. Because it is robust in these credible meanings, professionalism provides conceptual terrain for plausible claims by different segments of the bar to respectability and legitimacy.

Cause Lawyering as an Element of the Professional Project

Viewed in this way, professionalism is as meaningful, important, and accessible to cause lawyers as it is to dominant practitioners. It matters at least as much to lawyers struggling to gain acceptance as to those defending a position of privilege. In this context, professionalism is neither a set of essential attributes nor a singular tool produced and used by the powerful in a struggle to suppress the powerless. It is far too vague, complex, and contradictory to serve either purpose (Simon, 1984). Even the ABA Commission on Professionalism acknowledges, although it does not make much of it, that professionalism "is an elastic concept the meaning and application of which are hard to pin down" (1986: 10). Cause lawyering provides one form of contestation within the domain of lawyer professionalism, drawing sustenance from traditional assertions of the public role of the legal profession even as it challenges the core values associated with client service.

The story of the American Bar Association's shift from hostility toward cause lawyering to conditional acceptance has been compellingly told by Jerold Auerbach in his classic history of the legal profession, *Unequal Justice* (1976). This history helps us understand the way in which the ABA has attempted to selectively appropriate the social capital that accrues from the commitment of cause lawyers to use their legal skills for moral activism (Luban, 1988: xxii) while domesticating the practices of cause lawyers. By putting a humane face on lawyering, cause lawyers provide an appealing alternative to the value-neutral, "hired-gun" imagery that often dogs the legal profession.[3]

The wary alliance between cause lawyering and the organized legal profession is relatively recent. However, Auerbach (1976) provides an account of both the antecedents of the alliance and the antipathies to it within the professional culture of the nineteenth and the first half of the twentieth centuries. As for the alliance itself, Auerbach offers an illuminating look at its emergence in the turbulent years of the 1960s and 1970s. Throughout, Auerbach anchors his interpretation in an ongoing dialectic between lawyers allied to economic elites protecting organizational interests during times when they are under fire and those with a broader sense of professional responsibility (for another discussion of this dialectic, see Gordon, 1990).

We will draw on Auerbach's account as we examine the profession's uneasy and episodic embrace of cause lawyering. Briefly put, we argue that although this tenuous relationship can best be understood in instrumental terms, there is more to the story. On the one hand, the evidence indicates that cause lawyering has been less something to be valued in itself and more a vehicle for protecting organizational interests during times when they are under fire. However, during the years of the so-called rights revolution the composition of the organized legal profession underwent changes which made it and its conception of professional responsibility more receptive to cause lawyering.

The "Golden Age" of Civic Professionalism

There is considerable dispute about whether and when the legal profession in the United States enjoyed a "golden age"—and, indeed,
about what qualities should be associated with the professional gold
standard. Underlying the varying accounts of a golden age are competing visions of "civic professionalism" (Halliday, 1987) which in-
spire lawyers to make distinctive contributions to the well-being of
civil society (Gordon, 1984). In principle, there are as many versions
of civic professionalism as there are of the good society. In practice,
however, the competing visions of civic professionalism associated
with golden ages share the sense of a collective professional presence
deploying distinctively lawyerly resources to solve social and political problems.

For Auerbach, the so-called golden age of lawyering extended
from the founding of the Republic until the Civil War. In this era, the
profession was more or less at peace with itself. Although divided
between urban and country lawyers, the two segments of the profession complemented one another. From a broader perspective, this
was also an era of civic professionalism in which each segment of the
bar contributed in its own distinctive way to lawyering as a public
profession.[4]

Auerbach (1976: 16) depicts a "fragile synthesis" between the
"lawyer-aristocrats" identified by de Tocqueville and the "country
lawyers" represented historically by Abe Lincoln and in fiction by
Atticus Finch in *To Kill a Mockingbird*. "The country lawyer assured
equal opportunity, social mobility, and professional respectability for
the man of humblest origins, thereby preserving the democratic
flank of the profession. The aristocrat promised wealth and stature
for those who reached the top, thereby enhancing professional elit-
ism among those who served corporate business interests." Perforce
the country lawyer both knew and served the entire community in
small-town America. By choice, the lawyer aristocrat served the elite
and tended to identify with its interests and aspire to its privileged
position in the society. Lawyers argued that law itself provided a

"virtue-supplying substance" in the emerging commercial republic of the United States (Gordon, 1986: 11). Law, as they conceived it, was a "powerful autonomous culture . . . linking the specific interests of the 'different classes of the industrious' into a common general interest" (Gordon, 1986: 11).

Another way of describing the era of "fragile synthesis" is to characterize American lawyering as stratified, loosely organized, *but inclusive*. The different values and interests served by the country lawyers and lawyer aristocrats made the synthesis between them fragile. But what made the synthesis possible? In what sense was it inclusive? And why did it persist until, *but only until*, the latter decades of the nineteenth century?

To begin with, the profession itself was largely unorganized so that there was little or no interaction between country lawyers and lawyer aristocrats. Perhaps most significantly, apprenticeship training of fledgling lawyers allowed each segment of the profession to reproduce in its own image. Second, and most important in Auerbach's (1976) view, their common white, Anglo-Saxon, Protestant culture transcended the differences between lawyer aristocrats and country lawyers. Thus, the synthesis was inclusive in the sense that there was mutual recognition and acceptance across the political and financial divisions that stratified the bar in the early years of the Republic.

While there was no cause lawyering, as such, during this era, its civic professionalism did embrace two conceptions of the law as a public profession. The lawyer-aristocrats adopted the lawyer-statesman ideal discussed in the Chapter 1. "'While lawyers, and because we are lawyers, we are statesmen. . . . We are by profession statesmen' as Rufus Choate put it in a much quoted address on the 'Positions and Functions of the American Bar.'" (Gordon, 1986: 20). Simply put, from the Republic's beginning, lawyers have been disproportionately represented in American political institutions—in both elective and appointed positions (Miller, 1995).

The civic professionalism of the country lawyer was different. It is true that Lincoln and no doubt many other country lawyers shifted from legal practice to electoral politics. However, the country lawyer served civic professionalism simply by being available to most citizens. This is, in other words, the lawyer as peacemaker, discussed in the first chapter, who serves an integrative role for the community at large. Taken together, then, the two sides of Auerbach's "fragile synthesis" provided the *antecedents* of cause lawyering.

The Suppression of Civic Professionalism

Given the cultural homogeneity on which the fragile synthesis was founded, its collapse under the weight of the influx of non-WASP lawyers who were the product of the heavy immigration of late nineteenth and early twentieth centuries was predictable. There were a variety of reasons that elite lawyers saw non-WASP lawyers as a threat to the profession. By this time the professional elite had become closely allied with the emergent corporate sector—both as its lawyers and as its political allies (Gordon, 1983). The combination of this alliance and the threat posed by first-generation and second-generation lawyers generated a powerful synergy that led to the organization of the American Bar Association and to suppression of civic professionalism.

Why the aversion to these new-American lawyers? According to Auerbach (1976), there was, first and foremost, a strong nativist element operating—disdain by WASPs for the Catholics and Jews who were seen as invading and degrading the profession. In addition, the immigrants were closely associated with the political challenge mounted by reformers and revolutionaries to the corporation-backed Republican political ascendancy. Finally, these minority lawyers were overwhelmingly solo practitioners doing work that was seen as both trivial and disreputable. In contrast, the corporate lawyers celebrated their large firms, their exalted clients, and their challenging legal tasks. Note that the path chosen by the organized legal profession both reflected and contributed to the increasingly divisive stratification of American society during this period—stratification along the fault lines etched by class and ethnicity.

In any case, the schism within the profession became the organizing impetus of the ABA, which was, in effect, the official voice of the legal profession, the guardian of its ethnic purity, and the spearhead of an effort to make graduate education a condition of access to professional status. All of these activities of the ABA served the purpose of consolidating WASP control of the organized legal profession and allying it with corporate wealth (Auerbach, 1976: 65–73). To some extent, the process was direct and straightforward—the exclusion of African-Americans from the ABA and tenacious ABA opposition to Louis Brandeis's nomination to become the first Jewish justice on the U.S. Supreme Court. Much of it was, however, cloaked in a call for raising the ethical standards and the quality of expertise provided by lawyers to their clients. In ethical terms, for example, the ABA prohibited advertising and client solicitation as redolent of huckstering and beneath the dignity of true professionals. This was all well and good for corporate lawyers who could deploy their social networks to locate clients, but disabling to solo practitioners who had no such social capital at their disposal.

Most revealing and relevant to cause lawyering was a second fragile synthesis between the ABA and legal educators at elite universities. The ABA initiated a campaign of "ethnic cleansing" by mounting attacks on both apprenticeship training and night law schools. At the core of this campaign was the ostensibly neutral claim that the goal of legal education should be systematic training that was incompatible with the idiosyncrasies of apprenticeship. In order to make this case, Auerbach (1976) points out, it was necessary to establish not only that there was a generally accepted body of legal knowledge but also that this knowledge was appropriately associated with professional education for which undergraduate training was a necessary prerequisite. As Gordon (1986: 38, 40) argues, "The heart of the legal reform program (of the elite bar) was to build institutions capable of perfecting a national, general, uniform classical legal science . . . which gave these men a means of salvaging a cultural authority for law and lawyers that they experienced as in danger of subversion."

The result was an alliance between the ABA and legal educators—in particular, the legendary dean of the Harvard Law School, Christopher Columbus Langdell, and his pioneering case method of legal education. The case method was anchored in the claim that legal reasoning was a form of "scientific expertise" that could be taught in the classroom and enabled students, under the guidance of an academic expert, to distinguish valid from invalid legal decisions.

In the short term, this alliance with elite academic institutions and their faculty served the exclusionary purposes of the ABA, because in the late nineteenth and early twentieth centuries postsecondary education was overwhelmingly the province of social elites in the United States. Thus, insofar as a bachelor's degree was a prerequisite to legal education, the pool of applicants was narrowly circumscribed and further limited because postbaccalaureate training in law schools further added to the financial burden of becoming a lawyer. In addition, elite law schools became the recruitment conduit for the large Wall Street law firms that served big corporations. The immediate result was to reinforce the exclusionary stratification of the ABA and perforce to purge diversity from the organized legal profession. In Auerbach's words, "The emergence and proliferation of corporation law firms at the turn of the century provided those lawyers who possessed appropriate social, religious, and ethnic credentials with an opportunity to secure personal power and to shape their profession. . . . Only lawyers who possessed 'considerable *social* capital' could inhabit the corporate law firm world" (1976: 21–22). More broadly, the ABA, constituted by and under the control of Wall Street firms, purged democratic values from the profession. As Louis D. Brandeis, one of a relatively small number of leading lawyers who resisted this trend, put it in a 1905 speech to Harvard undergraduates, "Instead of holding a position of independence, between the wealthy and the people, prepared to curb the excesses of either, able lawyers have, to a great extent, allowed themselves to become adjuncts of great corporations and have neglected their obligation to use their powers for the protection of the people. We hear much of the 'corporate lawyer,' and far too little of the 'people's lawyers'" (quoted in Auerbach, 1976: 34–35).

Brandeis seems to use the term "people's lawyers" in two different ways. His primary argument is clearly that lawyers should serve as intermediaries between the affluent and the rest of the society. But the term *people's lawyer* also suggests a nonneutral position much closer to cause lawyering—a voice for the public in opposition to corporate interests. Either way, insofar as corporate firms controlled the ABA and insofar as these firms were in effect under the thumbs of their clients, the legal profession gave up the high ground of civic professionalism, which called for service to, and association with, a broad and inclusive social vision. Inextricably connected to corporate wealth and to corporate interests, the organized profession was no longer either autonomous or public. For Brandeis, this development both endangered the health of capitalist-democracy and the legitimacy of the legal profession (see Gordon, 1986: 47).

The Reemergence of Civic Professionalism

In the best tradition of the dialectic, the very success of the ABA's pervasive identification with the interests of corporate wealth carried with it the seeds of failure. The excesses of corporate wealth in the era of the "robber barons" generated political opposition ranging from socialists on the left to Bull Moose Republican reformers on the right. Not surprisingly, as corporations were increasingly discredited, so too were their lawyer allies. For reformers, as Auerbach (1976: 32) puts it, "the lawyer as surrogate for the corporation presented an alluring target." At the same time and for some of the same reasons the alliance between corporation law firms and legal academics began to weaken (Gordon, 1984: 75). Indeed, the legal academy became the seedbed of a renewed conception of, and commitment to, lawyering as a public profession.

To begin with, university education and legal training became more accessible—both ethnically and financially. In addition, the scientific expertise entrusted to academic lawyers took on democratic

overtones as legal academics looked beyond formal law to legal realism and the sociological jurisprudence of Roscoe Pound—with
their messages of reform and social engineering. Because legal education is the subject of Chapter 3, this is not the place to consider in
any detail the nature and evolution of legal education as it relates to
cause lawyering. However, it is impossible to understand the revival
of civic professionalism and its relationship to the bar's ambivalent
acceptance of cause lawyering without looking at the displacement
of Langdell's theory of law by legal realism.

Legal educators like Felix Frankfurter, influenced by Pound and
Brandeis, trained many of the young lawyers who joined the New
Deal and who became enthusiastic agents of the New Deal's social
and regulatory programs. Subsequently, many of these lawyers left
government service, went into private practice, and took on the representation of corporate clients in their dealings with government
regulators. The result was a Washington counterpart to New York's
Wall Street–oriented corporate firms. What formed was a kind of
companion legal elite with both the requisite educational pedigree
and corporate clients, but also with a background in public service
and an association with political reformers. Gordon (1986: 48) calls
these lawyers "bureaucratic statesmen." The result of their work was
not so much to reduce the stratification of the bar as to reshuffle the
elite and to introduce into it the democratic values and public-re-
garding professionalism that made the bar more receptive than it
would otherwise have been to the emergence of cause lawyering in
the 1960s and 1970s.

At its core, legal realism represented a demystification of formal
reasoning as the lifeblood of law. According to the realists, law was
the work of human beings who were driven by their interests, their
passions, and their values more than, or instead of, legal logic. Thus,
as Laura Kalman (1996: 13) points out, when Holmes claimed at the
turn of the twentieth century that the life of the law is "not logic but
experience," he captured the essence of legal realism but only hinted
at its program.

To get at the program, it is necessary to take a look at what
Holmes and the law professors who followed his cues meant by the

term *experience*—including both its negative and positive connotations. In negative terms, Holmes and the realists were intent on exposing the role of agency in judicial decision making and, more specifically, the extent to which conservative judges cloaked their preferences in general and their resistance to reform legislation in particular in the language of an objective legality. Brandeis understood experience in more positive terms. His goal, embodied in the "Brandeis brief" submitted in support of health and safety mandates for workers, was to bring sociological knowledge to bear on both legislative and judicial decisions.

A bevy of academic lawyers—Roscoe Pound at Harvard, John R. Commons at Wisconsin, Karl Llewellyn at Chicago, and Jerome Frank at Yale, to name just a few—proceeded to construct a realist jurisprudence. "Where traditional law professors exalted legal doctrine, realists spoke of 'integrating' law with political science, economics, anthropology, sociology, and linguistics" (Kalman, 1996: 16). As is readily inferable from the mix of disciplines mentioned by Kalman, realism was not so much a coherent theory as a mélange of predispositions for introducing the findings of the newly emergent social sciences into legal teaching, legal scholarship, legal process, and public policy.

During the 1930s, with the onset of the Great Depression and the coming of the New Deal, an ascendant legal realism contributed in a circuitous way to reinvigorate civic professionalism within the legal profession. As Kalman (1996: 13) points out, legal realism and political liberalism were "joined at the hip." The Great Depression served to discredit corporate lawyers, their corporate clients, and—most broadly—laissez-faire capitalism with its ideal of freedom from government. In contrast, New Deal liberals "reconceived the role of government in the political economy. . . . Relying on counter cyclical spending to promote consumption and employment, the federal government would 'create a compensatory welfare system (what later generations would call a "safety net") for those whom capitalism had failed' and intervene more aggressively to protect individual and civil rights" (Kalman, 1996: 15).

The New Deal in turn became a home, indeed a magnet, for

lawyers trained in realism and equipped to put social science at the service of the positive state. It is in this sense that the New Deal became very much (in the words of Auerbach) a "lawyers' deal" and service to the New Deal became a new form of civic professionalism. Felix Frankfurter, whose liberal credentials were stronger than his realist credentials, was especially renowned for inspiring his Harvard law students to serve the New Deal. In the short term, the pipeline between elite law schools and the New Deal revivified civic professionalism. As Ronen Shamir (1995: 173) notes:

The growing intervention of the state in the market created a new planning apparatus and offered new opportunities for legal academics and for a host of young lawyers who were educated in the realist spirit. It was through the door that the state opened in the New Deal that the realists were able to escape their alienation, to transgress the boundaries of the unifying paradigm in law, and to dictate an alternative agenda. Their critical discourse served the realists well. It allowed them to offer an alternative that suited the state's interest in moving from cases to causes, to legitimize new experiments as a kind of reasoned reflexivity, and, most importantly, to reshuffle the legal field's hierarchy in a way that assigned them a greater voice in reshaping the direction of legal development.

Thus, the New Deal created a parallel path of upward mobility in the legal profession—a path that was open to non-WASP lawyers who, despite their elite law school credentials, were not welcome in the big Wall Street firms which dominated the upper echelons of the ABA. Auerbach (1976: 184–85) puts it this way:

The New Deal did nothing to topple the Wall Street ladder; if anything it strengthened Wall Street firms by providing them with considerable additional business. But it did erect another ladder in Washington and invite Jewish lawyers to scramble for the highest rung. . . . Disproportionately concentrated at the top of their law school classes, they were disproportionately clustered at the bottom of the metropolitan bar. But the New Deal needed legal talent, and Jewish lawyers needed the jobs that the New Deal provided. Lawyers who defended unregulated corporate enterprise were predictably enraged to see young Jewish lawyers in Washington drafting and enforcing regulatory statutes against their clients.

In the long run, this government service "paid some lawyers a deferred dividend: ample financial rewards in private practice for the expertise developed in Washington" (Auerbach, 1976: 189). In other words, many of these New Deal lawyers went on to private practice in Washington representing corporate clients before the multiple agencies of the positive state. "The New Deal, ironically, had certified its own lawyers for careers in the service of those very clients who were most hostile to the Roosevelt administration" (Auerbach, 1976: 224).

It would, however, be incorrect to conclude that the most fundamental consequence of the creation of a parallel elite was to enhance the social mobility of minorities and to soften ethnic stratification with the bar. There was no retreat from the civic professionalism of the 1930s even after New Deal lawyers repaired to private practice and began representing corporate clients (Gordon, 1986: 55). To begin with, many of these Washington lawyers remained closely allied to, and often worked for and with, the liberal elite of the Democratic Party. In short, the influx of liberal-oriented legal realists to Washington established *a cohort of lawyer-statesmen.*

Still, as we argued in the previous chapter, lawyer-statesmen and cause lawyers are not at all the same thing. Indeed, Auerbach recounts the objections of the New Deal lawyers turned lawyer-statesmen—notably Abe Fortas and Lloyd Cutler—to the call for lawyers to take sides. "For these lawyers the morality of the adversary process must prevail: 'judgments of right and wrong,' Cutler insisted, 'are to be made after the process is completed, not before it begins'" (Auerbach, 1976: 281). Nonetheless, we will argue that the creation of a parallel elite of liberal lawyer-statesmen did contribute to the emergence of cause lawyering and to its ambivalent acceptance within the organized legal profession.

From Civic Professionalism to Cause Lawyering

The flow of lawyers from elite law schools into the New Deal and subsequently into a specialized Washington bar and the upper echelons of the legal profession tended to make the bar more responsive to the New Deal's egalitarian and interventionist values. As "the New Deal reshuffled elites within a hierarchical profession and society . . . from a corporate elite, served by Wall Street lawyers, to a legal elite, dominated by New Deal lawyers . . . ensconced in their Washington law firms" (Auerbach, 1976: 228), the profession became more receptive to realist understandings of law and of lawyers working on behalf of public purposes.

These were much the same understandings and values that were in the 1960s and 1970s to drive the work of cause lawyers on behalf of racial justice, the antipoverty programs of the Great Society, the antiwar movement, and a variety of other reforms. In addition, these same Washington law firms were supportive of pro bono programs that enabled young lawyers to work for a variety of causes while retaining their "day jobs" representing corporate clients before government agencies (Rhode, 2000a). They were thus able to remain on track for lucrative partnerships—doing well while doing good.

We are not, it is important to emphasize, arguing that cause lawyering began in the 1960s and 1970s. Certainly, the work of the NAACP and the ACLU can be traced to the turn of the twentieth century and the immediate post–World War I periods, respectively. The National Lawyers Guild was an aggressive advocate of social justice beginning in the 1930s, and its lawyers also mobilized in support of the victims of McCarthyism in the 1950s. It was, however, we contend, not until the 1960s and 1970s that cause lawyering made a kind of peace with the organized bar and became a substantial presence within the profession. How, why, and to what extent did this happen?

Auerbach (1976) attributes a change of heart within the professional elite to a "sustained crisis of professionalism" brought on by the profession's dubious role in three of the defining events of the decades from the mid-1950s to the mid-1970s. To begin with, there was the reluctance of government attorneys in the Eisenhower administration to engage in vigorous enforcement of the Supreme Court's school desegregation decisions. The result was the spectacle of "massive resistance" to desegregation rulings of the courts—including most notoriously the failure to respond legally to the murder, intimidation, and degradation of schoolchildren and civil rights demonstrators. Instead of enforcing rights, government lawyers chose for almost a decade to defer to "federalism, individualism, legalism and professionalism" (Auerbach, 1976: 267). Also egregiously problematic was the orchestration of the Watergate cover-up by President Nixon's lawyers—by John Dean and John Ehrlichman, in particular. Finally, there was the opposition of the ABA, led by future Supreme Court justice Lewis Powell, to the creation of a nationally funded legal services program and to its social justice objectives.

Auerbach (1976: 263) concludes that these events led to a disintegration of "faith in legal authority" and, in particular, to an inclination to associate the organized legal profession with social injustice. Well-known and influential lawyers were seen to be disproportionately on the wrong side in these issues, not because of their individual idiosyncrasies but as a consequence of prevailing professional ethics and practices. Lawyers, according to this way of thinking, privileged procedure over substance and made themselves available as "hired guns" irrespective of the intrinsic merits of the claims and clients that they represented. From the point of view of the organized profession this was a classic example of the public's tendency to confuse morality with ethics.

From a different point of view, this was an instance of professional degradation, not unlike the profession's unwavering support of, and inextricable association with, unregulated, laissez-faire capitalism at the turn of the twentieth century. In other words, the profession once again found itself on the wrong side of an emergent public discourse. As the public became increasingly receptive to egalitarian reforms and to the privileging of human rights over property rights, it viewed the conventional "professionalism" of the ABA as contributing to "social injustice" (Auerbach, 1976: 268).

Auerbach is no doubt correct in concluding that all of this apparent chicanery contributed to a disintegration of legal authority, but from our point of view what is more noteworthy is the somewhat ironic contribution of these developments to a reinvigoration of faith in the law as an instrument of social, political, and economic reform. Lawyers, it is true, can reasonably be held responsible for orchestrating the Watergate cover-up, for the evasion of desegregation decrees, and for opposing the creation of a legal services program dedicated to social justice. However, law and lawyers were also instrumental in efforts to uncover the cover-up of Watergate and to impeach President Nixon. Similarly, it was NAACP lawyers who generated civil rights litigation and the preeminent institution of legal authority, the U.S. Supreme Court, which handed down the desegregation decisions (Kluger, 1975). Finally, it was lawyers who led the campaign to establish an antipoverty-oriented legal services program. In short, as is so often the case in the United States, lawyers could be found in the forefront of all sides of these issues.

The so-called disintegration of legal authority thus became the occasion for a climate of reform in which cause lawyers became increasingly prominent. Their prominence emerged out of a convergence of three forces: Lyndon Johnson's Great Society program, the egalitarian jurisprudence of the Warren Court, and the intellectual and pedagogical initiative of academic lawyers. Most broadly, the Great Society program established a comprehensive egalitarian political agenda. More specifically, its legal services program funded the work of lawyers with ambitions not only to provide legal representation for the poor but also to attack the root causes of poverty (Cahn and Cahn, 1964). The Warren Court's receptivity to reform litigation suggested that cause lawyers could successfully pursue an egalitarian agenda. Taken together, as Laura Kalman (1996: 43) points out, "Legalists, such as Johnson and Warren, assumed that most of the 'flaws' in American society could and would be corrected through legal means. They had faith in the immanent liberalism of legal institutions and equated 'law' with 'freedom' and 'equality.'"

While Kalman's characterization of Lyndon Johnson and Earl Warren as legalists is correct, their legalism should also be seen as an elemental artifact of the prevailing political culture in the United States—first and most memorably observed by de Tocqueville. Kalman's (1996: 49) more specific point is that, much as in the New Deal era, realist academic lawyers were constructing an intellectual case for law and lawyers who were taking the egalitarian initiative.

For their part, law students, Auerbach (1976: 277) tells us, began "to insist upon professional training that would at least acknowledge, if not cultivate, the exercise of conscience and commitment by individual attorneys." Law faculties were more than happy to oblige. According to Kalman (1996: 52), "Law schools capitalized on the Warren Court. 'Glossy admission brochures entice some students into law school with promises that lawyers of the future, riding white chargers, will crusade against social problems,' one student wrote."

The upshot of all of this ferment was that cause lawyers became increasingly prominent—as agents not only of civil rights and anti-poverty work but also on behalf of consumer protection, environmental cleanup, the antiwar movement, feminism, and a variety of other campaigns for human rights and social justice. Nonetheless, it would be an overstatement to conclude that cause lawyers as a result became equal partners within the legal profession.

It is fair to say, however, that cause lawyers did gain substantial leverage within the profession and that they had remarkable success in litigating on behalf of an ambitious reform agenda. In this liberal political climate, the organized profession was generally receptive to cause lawyers—at least to those working close to the liberal mainstream. Young idealistic lawyers were a welcome addition to a profession fighting a rearguard action against the lawyerly sins of the Watergate era. Indeed, corporate firms felt compelled by the competition for the best and the brightest to create in-firm cause lawyering opportunities—in the form of pro bono programs and street-level clinics in poverty-stricken urban areas.

More directly, young lawyers competed intensely for positions with nongovernmental reform organizations (e.g., Ralph Nader's

Public Citizen, various environmental organizations, and the like). Public Citizen's reform campaign was directed primarily at vigorous regulatory enforcement of consumer and environmental protection laws. As for the legal services program, its ambitious objectives and unconventional methods were strongly appealing to young cause lawyers.

Perhaps most emblematic of these latter objectives was Gary Bellow's California Rural Legal Assistance Program, which drew the ire of powerful agribusiness interests in California and resulted in an assault on the legal services program led by ex-Hollywood personalities Senator George Murphy and Governor Ronald Reagan. While this and subsequent attacks were successful in curbing antipoverty ambitions—markedly shrinking the size and encroaching on the independence of legal services—the program was saved in no small measure because of the efforts of the American Bar Association. This episode and its ambivalent outcome reveal both the professional respectability of cause lawyering and the limits of its professional acceptance.

The Fragile Alliance Redux

As the broader political culture became more conservative after 1980, as the market for legal services became more competitive, and as moral advocacy lost its luster for most young lawyers, the profession's receptivity to cause lawyering diminished. At the level of the firm, as we will detail in later chapters, bottom-line concerns eroded support for cause lawyering, with its tendency to eat into billable hours and sap the energies of young associates. As for the organized profession, it continued to call for vigorous pro bono programs and to support government-funded legal services.

However, the legal services program has been weakened despite the constant support of the ABA. Similarly, there is little or no reason to believe that ABA resolutions on behalf of pro bono programs had any significant effect on firms. Indeed, as we will explain subsequently, pro bono programs have increasingly emphasized firm development—service to nonprofits associated with civic elites and, therefore, to potential clients, rather than to social justice (Cummings, 2004).

Yet in the last decades of the twentieth century the organized bar continued its fragile toleration of cause lawyers, forging temporary alliances rather than fundamentally altering its understanding of the relationship of professionalism and politics. Emblematic is the ABA's effort to support lawyering against the death penalty (Sarat, 2001).

In the mid-1980s, responding to the earlier reinstatement of the death penalty and the growing number of persons on death row, the Congress of the United States authorized the creation of capital defense resource centers to be operated by the Administrative Office of the Courts. Similar operations were approved and funded by a few state legislatures (see O'Brien, 1990; Ruthenbeck, 1989; Lacayo, 1992). One purpose of these centers was to help identify and train private lawyers to handle the appellate and postconviction stages of capital litigation for persons under a sentence of death and, where it was impossible to do so, to provide direct representation themselves. By the end of the 1980s, resource centers were operating in thirteen of the more than thirty states which authorized death as a punishment.

Over the next several years those centers played a key role in the death penalty bar (Sarat, 1998a). Because the lawyers who worked in them were better paid than anti–death penalty lawyers in public interest settings and because they had more resources at their disposal, they quickly became critically important in the network of anti–death penalty lawyering around the country, providing advice, information, and even personnel to battle individual death sentences and to develop strategy in the ongoing fight against capital punishment. And, over time, while they made little headway against the death penalty itself, they were very successful in delaying executions, so much so that it seemed for a time as if capital punishment in the United States would exist at the level of a judicially imposed sentence rather than an actually implemented punishment (Gross, 1993).

By the early 1990s, however, the political tide had swung ever more vehemently to the right on criminal justice issues, and the political fervor to see that death sentences were carried out intensified. When the Republicans took control of the Congress in January 1995, one of their first targets was federal funding for capital defense resource centers (Berkman, 1995). The centers were criticized for engaging in guerrilla warfare on behalf of death row inmates and for moving beyond legal representation into politics, for moving from client to cause lawyering (Amsterdam, 1998). Despite a spirited defense of the resource centers by the American Bar Association, in the spring of 1995 Congress refused to reauthorize or fund the resource centers as of October 1, 1996.

The reaction of the American Bar Association to this decision is a key indicator of the unstable equilibrium in which cause lawyers exist, and it provides an important vehicle for exploring the legitimation politics of cause lawyering in the liberal state. It also exemplifies the intense competition to influence the state's investment in symbolic capital in a neoliberal era. Key to understanding the ABA's reaction and its strategy in this competition was the passage of a resolution in February 1997 (American Bar Association, 1997) calling for a moratorium on the carrying out of the death penalty in the United States. This resolution is an instance of "abolitionism as legal conservatism" (Sarat, 1998b) and an indication of the way the bar both needs and defends, while seeking to domesticate, cause lawyering.

In its resolution, the ABA proclaimed that the death penalty as currently administered is not compatible with central values of our Constitution. Thus the American Bar Association (1997: 1) "calls upon each jurisdiction that imposes capital punishment not to carry out the death penalty until the jurisdiction implements policies and procedures . . . intended to (1) ensure that death penalty cases are administered fairly and impartially, in accordance with due process, and (2) minimize the risk that innocent people may be executed." The ABA's resolution represented the culmination of a twenty-year history of ABA activism on death penalty issues. That the ABA intervened as it did and that it allied itself with a small group of cause lawyers adamantly opposed to capital punishment resulted from the conjunction of the decision by the Congress of the United States, certain justices of the Supreme Court, and certain members of the political class at both the state and federal level to disinvest in policies and symbols which in their view were associated with a growing crisis of capacity and legitimacy and, second, the ability of abolitionists and their allies in the ABA to cast the vote on the moratorium resolution in the language of civic professionalism. What some perceived as a sudden and radical shift of the state's symbolic capital away from legality precipitated an alliance between the organized bar and anti–death penalty lawyers. In that alliance, cause lawyers could assume the position of legal conservatives rather than political radicals.

Here is one instance in which "technical issues become political issues . . . [and] professionals become public moralists" (Halliday, 1987: 39). When this occurs, when the symbolic capital of the organized bar is most in question, the leverage of civic professionalism in the struggle over the state's deployment of its symbolic capital would seem to be most attenuated. Thus the alliance of the ABA and cause lawyers fighting the death penalty would itself seem to be a fragile and unstable one, beneficial to the latter in shoring up its morale and providing some important political resources, beneficial to the former in asserting the political claims of professional authority.

But, despite these benefits, this alliance was not without its costs. From the perspective of the ABA the most significant of those costs might be a further diminution of its claims to authority based solely on technical expertise; from the perspective of the death penalty bar, the cost of its alliance with the ABA is a possible erosion in its commitment to political and social transformation as well as a deepening of fissures among its members.

The ABA's embrace of cause lawyering in the context of capital punishment reveals the role that cause lawyers may play in legitimating liberal legality precisely by vigorously challenging particular state policies. In this embrace, and in others like it, the organized bar seeks to extend and alter the time horizon of the state beyond the immediate push to satisfy politically noisy constituencies, to redirect it to attend to the continuing need to live up to, or at least to appear to live up to, the central promises of liberal legalism (see Sarat, 1998a). The ABA's response to the defunding of death penalty resource centers and the attack on habeas corpus reveals a persistent, unalleviated anxiety about the uses and disposition of its own symbolic capital. Fairness, due process, equal protection—values vigorously defended by the anti–death penalty bar—help protect that capital. To attack lawyers serving persons on death row, the ABA seemed to say, may be politically attractive in the short run but will, over time, be counterproductive.

Thus, the organized bar's defense of cause lawyers was, in this instance, equated with a defense of law itself. When pressures in the political process are such that the state seems to be disinvesting its symbolic capital in certain understandings of legality, the bar may use its own symbolic capital in ways that support cause lawyers and cause lawyering, even when those lawyers work for causes as politically unpopular as the abolition of the death penalty is in the United States. Cause lawyering was in this instance, as it has been in others, essential both in the struggle over where and how the liberal state's symbolic capital would be invested and in the reproduction of liberal legality itself.

Conclusion

The story recounted in this chapter explains how, why, and to what extent cause lawyering has been able to secure a foothold, however tenuous, within the legal profession's dominant culture. It is not primarily the story of a change of heart by the organized bar, but instead a consequence of contingent and historically specific strategic action in response to threats to the profession's own social capital. While it is true that the infiltration of the elite in the middle of the twentieth century by New Deal lawyers altered the rigidly conservative ethos of the professional culture, there is little or no reason to believe, despite the complaints of conservative commentators, that the organized bar has been suddenly transformed into a hotbed of liberalism—nor for that matter of liberal legalism.

Much more important in our judgment were the profession's efforts to alter its reputation by capitalizing on the luster of cause lawyering, the egalitarian values pursued by cause lawyers, and the bar's own interventions on behalf of legality itself. Today the organized profession is no longer as hostile to cause lawyering as it once certainly was. Gone are the days when the president of the ABA could, as did Lewis Powell in the 1960s, challenge the ethical foundation of cause lawyering: "His insistence upon fidelity to traditional ethics threatened to undercut the basic purposes of the [legal services] program; for strict adherence to the inhibitions [to partisan representation] incorporated in the Canons [of Professional Responsibility] would contribute to the very problems that the OEO was created to resolve" (Auerbach, 1976: 271). As Auerbach (1976: 275) points out, the work of civil rights and antipoverty lawyering in the 1950s, 1960s, and 1970s has effectively "expanded definitions of professional responsibility." To some limited extent, cause lawyering has, in other words, been incorporated into the bar's definition of civic professionalism.[5] No longer is it limited to the activities of latter-day lawyer-aristocrats and country lawyers—that is, to lawyers working part time as statesmen and to lawyers working to reduce and resolve conflict. The profession accommodates lawyers who construct their practices around the goals of serving causes and targeting clients whose cases further causes which the lawyers favor—at least so long as those causes act within the domain of liberal-legality.

It is, however, one thing to accept or tolerate cause lawyering, especially that brand which most wholeheartedly embraces liberal democratic rights, and quite another to embrace and promote cause lawyering which serves other ideas of democracy. The distress of the 1960s and 1970s led the bar to embrace cause lawyering. In recent years, however, the political climate has changed, and the organized profession has tended to retreat to a position of toleration marked by occasional episodes of vigorous defense. In tandem with its waning enthusiasm for cause lawyering in general, the organized bar has tended to narrow its definition of what constitutes legitimate cause lawyering.

There is still another way to understand and explain the profession's conditional support for cause lawyering. As we have argued, the emergence of cause lawyering can be reasonably traced historically to the convergence of realist jurisprudence and New Deal politics. As such, cause lawyering has been very much a creature of legalism *and* liberalism. Auerbach (1976) might well argue that the traditional support of the organized legal profession and elite lawyers for corporate enterprise constituted in fact, if not in form, cause lawyering on the right. However, as we pointed out in Chapter 1, it was only on the left that lawyering for a cause was explicitly acknowledged and defended. Conservatives, in contrast, have *until recently* denied that they were engaged in advocacy that transcended neutral client service in any way.

These days the profession's understanding of what constitutes legitimate cause lawyering is undergoing a significant transformation. On the one hand, the profession seems to be distancing itself from some dimensions of liberalism—with its acceptance of a legalistic apolitical agenda for legal services being a case in point. On the other hand, there is no comparable evidence of the profession backing away from the increasingly self-conscious and assertive conservative cause lawyering that has emerged over the last couple of decades in opposition to abortion and gun control, in support of prayer in the public school, and the like. Consider also the conflict over tort reform within and beyond the profession, in which conservative legal foundations supported by corporate funding vilify the trial lawyers who challenge corporate wrongdoing.

We return to all of this in greater detail in Chapter 5, where we consider the multiple faces of democratic advocacy among cause lawyers. Yet we can say here that from the perspective of the organized legal profession the nature of and the support for cause lawyering continues to be contested, and the outcome of this contestation remains very much in doubt.

CHAPTER 3

Beating the Odds: Cause Lawyering
and Legal Education

LEGAL EDUCATION is the domain in which the conventional, client-centered ethos of lawyering is perhaps most fully and regularly expressed (Schneyer, 2002). Learning to think like a lawyer means learning to leave one's personal moral and political views behind, to think analytically about the fit between facts and rules (Noonan, 1976). Learning to think like a lawyer means learning to think beyond one's preferences and developing the skill of identifying the best arguments on all sides of disputed questions. As Karl Llewellyn (1960: 84) described it,

[The first year of law school] aims, in the old phrase, to get you to "think like a lawyer." The hardest job of the first year is to lop off your common sense, to knock your ethics into temporary anesthesia. Your view of social policy, your sense of justice—to knock these out of you along with woozy thinking, along with ideas all fuzzed along the edges. You are to acquire the ability to think precisely, to analyze coldly, to see, and see only, and manipulate the machinery of law. It is not easy thus to turn human beings into lawyers.

If cause lawyers find in their practice an opportunity to lead an unalienated professional life, to find something to believe in, it would seem to be in spite, rather than because, of what they learn in law school (Wizner, 2001, 2002).

Critics of the mainstream "think-like-a-lawyer" brand of legal education abound. These critics include law professors (Stevens, 1983), academic researchers (Sarat, 1993), and untold numbers of law students—some of whom have written persuasively about the tribulations and satisfactions of legal education (e.g., Goodrich, 1991; Kahlenberg, 1992). One of these former students (Goodrich, 1991: 115, 95), echoing Llewellyn, reflects on his experience at Yale Law School: "Law made me less human, asked that I dismiss my moral center as a dangerous, incomprehensible Pandora's box. . . . If life is a jigsaw puzzle, the lawyer's job is to place a handful of pieces on the table and convince his viewers they saw a complete picture."

There are clear political themes in many of these critiques. *On the left*, the basic charge is that built into the conventional version of legal education is a professional and political alliance between elite law schools and the upper echelons of professional, corporate, and political privilege. To remedy this imbalance, some critics have called for an increased emphasis on "public interest" perspectives in legal education (see, e.g., Rhode, 1999). In their view, learning to think like a lawyer has its parallel in the choice of what kind of law to practice, and it turns out that the vocational lessons of legal education are the same as its classroom pedagogy, namely to renounce idealism, conform to standard professional aspirations, and, in so doing, separate one's professional life from one's personal commitments. The overriding purpose of legal education is to ready lawyers for disinterested client service, training them in the hired-gun ethos favored by corporate firms. Law schools identify and train the best and brightest law students to become compliant (and well-paid) cogs in those firms—"legal education as training for hierarchy," in the words of Harvard law professor Duncan Kennedy (1982).

Critics *on the right* detect a different kind of hidden agenda in legal education. They argue that beneath Llewellyn's version of legal education stirs a set of political preferences that animate the law school curriculum. At the heart of this conservative critique is the claim that for too many law professors, law is no longer a vocation but a means to other ends—mostly self-aggrandizement and social advocacy (Kronman, 1993). According to this way of thinking, wayward academics—"Rambo scholars," in the words of Mary Ann Glendon (1994), Kennedy's Harvard colleague—pass on to students all of the wrong messages. Critics point to statements like the following: "We need to profess a social, political and moral agenda in our teaching, an agenda that exposes students to the mal-distribution of wealth, power, and rights in society, and that seeks to inculcate in them a sense of their own ability and responsibility for using law to challenge injustice" (Wizner, 2002: 331). Such assertions are taken by conservative critics as evidence of biased teaching—revealing both a thinly concealed message that law should be put at the service of liberal values and a neglect of traditional lawyerly virtues like competence, sagacity, and honesty.

Critics differ sharply on both the problems with legal education and on how to solve them. There is, however, substantial agreement on four things—although not necessarily on whether they are virtues or vices.

1. Legal education sharpens *intellectual skills* by enhancing the capacity for rigorous rational thought.
2. Law school profoundly alters not only the intellect but the *personality* as well.
3. Legal education is of dubious value in preparing students for *legal practice.*
4. The law school experience enhances appreciation of liberal democratic *rights.*

However one characterizes legal education, one thing seems indisputably true. For many students, interest in cause lawyering careers declines sharply during law school. The focus of this book is, of course, on that subset of students whose commitment to cause lawyering survives legal education. However, to fully appreciate the tensions and ambivalent relationship between cause lawyering and the professional project of the organized bar, it is necessary to understand law school's powerful socializing messages—privileging private practice in general and elite law firms in particular and privileging, as well, analytic distance rather than political commitment. We begin by documenting what many (e.g., Stover, 1989) have described as a progressive disenchantment with cause lawyering over the course of legal education.

The Retreat from Cause Lawyering

Many students "enter law school determined to use law to promote liberal ideals and leave three years later to counsel the least socially progressive elements of our society" (Kahlenberg, 1992: 5). By the end of law school, it turns out that "jobs with large private law firms are the most sought after positions by most American law school graduates" (Lempert, Chambers, and Adams, 2000: 424). Empirical research (Erlanger et al., 1996; Erlanger and Klegon, 1978; Foster, 1981, 1985; Granfield and Koenig, 1992a, 1992b; Wilkens, 1987) consistently reveals the kind of diminished interest in cause lawyering during law school that Richard Kahlenberg (1992) describes.[1]

These data have been collected at a variety of different kinds of law schools—including one law school whose self-described mission is to awaken and nurture the values associated with cause lawyering. Robert Stover's (1989) findings as a participant-researcher at the University of Denver Law School are typical. He observed, over the course of three years of legal education, "My classmates' desire to practice public interest law decreased significantly. . . . For example, the 33% who in the fall of 1977 chose a public interest job (from my list of twenty) as most preferable for an initial full-time job shrank by half. And the number of public interest jobs rated among the top five on the list fell from three to one" (Stover, 1989: 3).

Robert Granfield's (1992: 38) research at Harvard qualifies Stover's findings, but without changing the overall picture of a *three-year retreat from cause lawyering*. Granfield asked students to rank-order a list of thirteen motivations for attending law school and discovered that just over a quarter of the class was motivated by altruistic goals which included helping people, promoting social justice, and pursuing social change. Conversely, about 40 percent were driven by such conventional vocational goals as money, social status, and career enhancement. Cause lawyering objectives were the second and third choices of roughly another 35 percent of the entering class. The same objectives were still alive at the conclusion of the third year—but just barely—when "only 2 percent [of those students who responded] indicated a preference for legal aid jobs and only 5 percent were still considering public interest jobs" (Granfield, 1992: 48).

Granfield's (1992: 184–85) ancillary research at Northeastern University Law School underscores just how consistent is the tale of disaffection with cause lawyering over the three years of legal education.[2] As Granfield puts it, "The ideological role of . . . [Northeastern] Law School was to be consistent with the values reflected by 1960s social activists; students would be trained for the goal of providing legal services to the poor, minorities, and oppressed social groups" (Granfield 1992: 173). In short, it would not be a stretch to say that the primary objective at Northeastern was to produce cause lawyers.

Given this goal, it is hardly surprising that Northeastern attracted to its entering class a higher proportion of students with cause lawyering commitments. More surprising is a retreat from cause lawyering which is indistinguishable from what researchers have reported at other schools. Northeastern students complained of many of the same things as did students elsewhere—the hyperrationality of legal education, its emphasis on adversarial advocacy, the emotional toll it takes, and so on. Nonetheless, Northeastern students became less interested in resolving social problems, in social change more generally, and less interested in doing pro bono work. Those students reporting enhanced interest in pro bono dropped off from 69 percent at the end of the first year to 38 percent and 44 percent at the end of the second and third years respectively (Granfield, 1992: 185).

Despite all their apparent good intentions, the faculty at Northeastern continued to teach in ways that were largely indistinguishable from the conventional legal pedagogy. In order to maintain its academic legitimacy, the school remained committed to teaching students to "think like lawyers." The conventional pedagogy prevailed with its emphasis on the case method, fabricating persuasive arguments, and suppressing issues of social justice. As one student put it, reflecting on what she had learned at Northeastern, "Opportunities to promote social change through law are extremely limited" (Granfield, 1992: 185).

The retreat from cause lawyering at Northeastern was also abetted by its success in placing students in elite law firms. These placements were especially difficult for the typical Northeastern student to resist. Whereas at schools like Harvard elite placements were viewed more or less as entitlements, at Northeastern they were seen as affirmations of both the students and the institution. Granfield (1992: 192) reports that "one thirty-two-year-old woman who had entered law school to do public interest law described her large firm job as the great American success story. 'It makes me proud,' she said, 'to know that I'm good enough to be hired at a large law firm like this.'" As a result of such sentiments, there was a substantial divide between the students seeking upward mobility and those with commitments to cause lawyering.

Students from schools like Northeastern are more likely to come to elite law firms and to private practice as supplicants rather than as entitled novices. They are likely to be less certain of success and more compliant—less likely to seek pro bono commitments from their firms and, indeed, less willing to take on the added burden of pro bono activities. As a result, students at Northeastern experienced a precipitous drop-off from initially high levels of interest in resolving social problems, in social change, and in public interest work. There, as at Harvard, Denver, and elsewhere, as legal education progressed, idealism regressed.

It is, of course, one thing to establish that interest in cause lawyering dwindles during the three years of law school and quite another to explain why that is the case or to establish a cause-and-effect relationship between legal education and the retreat from cause lawyering. Craig Kubey (1976) argues, for example, that a variety of other factors are better predictors of interest in cause lawyering than legal education. In addition, research conducted at the University of Wisconsin concluded that interest in cause lawyering waxes and wanes in response to the job market. Thus, cause lawyering was much more attractive in the 1960s and early 1970s when such positions were plentiful than subsequently as they became increasingly scarce (Erlanger et al., 1996; Erlanger and Klegon, 1978).

Similarly, there is reason to believe that interest in cause lawyering varies with changes in the political climate. Just as lawyers flocked to the New Deal in the 1930s, so too did lawyers enter cause lawyering in greater numbers in the heady days of the 1960s and 1970s—and for reasons not necessarily connected to the job market. These latter-day corporate refuseniks were inspired, as we argued earlier, by the successes and heroism of civil rights lawyers, by a progressive rights-driven political ethos, and by the receptivity of the courts, especially the Warren Court, to rights claims.

Thus, David Chambers (n.d.) reports that the percentage of University of Michigan Law School graduates entering a variety of public interest and public service jobs climbed steadily from the mid-1960s (8 percent) through much of the 1970s, reaching a high of 17 percent for those graduating in 1975 and 1976. By 1987–88, the percentage had dropped to 2 percent. More comprehensive data, gathered by the National Association for Law Placement, reveal that the numbers of students going into public interest law dropped by almost 50 percent between 1978 and 1988 (reported in Granfield, 1992: 5).

Whatever the influence of factors like the job market and the prevailing political ethos, something seems to happen during the law school years to dampen student enthusiasm for cause lawyering. But how and why does legal education work against cause lawyering? In part, it does so by ignoring the difficulties of sustaining the commitments that bring many students to law school (Abel, 2002). Because of its value as a form of ideological legitimation, cause lawyering figures prominently in the welcoming ceremonies for new students and again at graduation exercises. Yet little attention is paid to it in between. Instead, students face repeated indoctrination in the conventional ethos of client-oriented lawyering. This omission led Stover (1989: 1) to characterize the status of cause lawyering in legal education as "bookends without books."

When law schools are not ignoring cause lawyering, they often express hostility toward it. Accordingly, with the help of Granfield's (1992) findings, we offer an explanation of the consistent record of disaffection from cause lawyering—an explanation that is different from Stover's (1989) but not in conflict with it. That explanation begins with an examination of the intense and transformative impact of legal education on students' understandings of what it means to be a lawyer.

Producing Professionals

Chris Goodrich (1991) claims that the impact of legal education is cognitive, emotional, and moral. The transformations that he describes in his account of his own law school experience have been echoed by a host of others who have taught in or attended law school,[3] including best-selling author and lawyer Scott Turow (1977) and Harvard law professor Duncan Kennedy (1982), as well as many other lesser-known figures.[4] Virtually all of them trace the changes wrought by legal education to the process of teaching students how to think like lawyers—and to the moral and emotional repercussions of that cognitive conversion. The dominant view is that moral sensibilities are weakened or even extinguished by legal education, that political commitment is regarded as a barrier, not an aid, to making good lawyers.

Yet law students may not lose their ideals during their legal education; instead, moral ideals and political commitments are exiled to the private realm and replaced by ideals that are intrinsic to legal practice. Granfield's (1992) formulation of this change suggests a distinction, which, as we argued in Chapter 1, is fundamental to cause lawyering. Recall our claim that both cause and conventional lawyers have ideals, but that for conventional lawyers these ideals are ethical while for cause lawyers they are moral or political. Although Granfield (1992) does not distinguish between ethics and morals, he does demonstrate that students who retreat from an initial commitment to cause lawyering develop an alternative idealism—the commitment to disinterested client service—an idealism which is, in effect, constructed within the existing ethical precepts of the legal profession.

Students come to legal education, as one student put it, "looking for answers" (Granfield, 1992: 54), only to find that legal education is really about "creative argumentation" (Granfield, 1992: 56). This leads many students to think of law as "just a game" (Granfield, 1992: 63). Survival involves "adjusting . . . idealism to gamesmanship . . . [and] culminates not in a loss of values, but rather in a redefinition of students' nascent views about justice and social activism" (Granfield, 1992: 61).

Law students discover "an ideology of pragmatism" (Granfield, 1992: 61). They learn that insofar as they inject their personal moral judgments into cases they confuse matters still further—and to no avail. As one student explained, "I was so wrapped up with the people in the case that I totally missed what the legal issue was" (Granfield, 1992: 77). More broadly, as Granfield (1992: 74) puts it, "If legal education teaches anything it teaches aspiring lawyers that there are no simple answers, only simplistic solutions."

Students learn "to see and accept the boundaries within the law and legal discourse" (Granfield, 1992: 85). The result is a new and different kind of moral awareness anchored in a recognition of "the true complexity of social relations and social policy questions"—and, thus, "an emerging morality considered superior to the mundane morality of the private citizen" (Granfield, 1992: 74). In sum, "students learn to define their initial perspectives concerning law and society as markedly inferior to their newly honed legal views" (Granfield, 1992: 74) and, in any case, incompatible with effective legal advocacy.

Insofar as law and legal practice are deemed incompatible with political action, better to separate one from the other. As Granfield

(1992: 87) paraphrases one student's strategy, "she could practice commercially-oriented law within a capitalist framework while preserving her idealism through activities in her private life."[5] Whether this is deemed making a virtue of necessity or is seen as moral transformation (rather than as moral capitulation), it helps explain how and why legal education tends to be inhospitable to cause lawyering but not necessarily to the kinds of idealism associated with the role of lawyer-statesman or with doing one's bit for equal representation.

Students learn about deploying rights as a tool of the trade of conventional legal practice. Accordingly, to put that tool to work part time and do pro bono on behalf of the constitutional rights of prisoners, the unborn, racial minorities, property owners, and so on is altogether consistent with widely accepted professional practice. Despite occasional instances of robust cause lawyering, pro bono is more about giving something back than about commitment to a cause—about providing for unmet legal needs, about affirming liberal democratic values, and about upholding the highest ethical standards of legal practice. In short, pro bono lawyering is more about adversary justice than social justice.[6]

The Cognitive Core

The core purpose and major achievement of legal education is to retool the way students think. As we have already noted, thinking like a lawyer requires that students substitute an allegedly objective, precise, and rational mode of thought for value-laden, emotional, and politically driven habits of mind. Built around the case method, the law school curriculum is still dominated by the study of precedent-setting cases in various branches of the law—contracts, torts, property, and so on. Ordinarily, these cases are presented historically, with the students learning how and why the law has evolved—with precedents being set and revised over the years.

In Christopher Columbus Langdell's original formulation, law at its best was said to be driven exclusively by a rigorous and relentless logic, which led toward, without ever quite achieving, a coherent, comprehensive, and essentially seamless system of rules. The advent of legal realism (Peller, 1985), with its exposure of an indeterminacy intrinsic to legal logic and its insistence on experience rather than logic as the driving force of law, shook the Langdell paradigm but did not displace it (Schneyer, 2002). On the one hand, realists continued to strive for an ever more coherent system, although the locus of realist coherence was *empirical*, more than logical, truth. Whereas Langdell put his faith in philosophy, the realists put theirs in social science.[7] Either way, the goal was to provide students with an ascertainable standard of validity. Moreover, the realists did not abandon logic. Instead, they developed approaches in which logic and experience were brought together in eclectic and idiosyncratic ways according to the inclinations of individual instructors.

With virtually all law teachers providing their own distinctive elixirs of realism and Langdellian legalism, students get multiple messages about what it is to think like a lawyer. Rather than divulging the rules of the new game by which students are expected to play, instructors require that students infer the rules from purposefully confusing classroom discussions of the multiplicity of cases covered in each of their first-year classes. As Rhode (2000b: 197) puts it, "Under conventional Socratic approaches, the professor controls the dialogue, invites the students to 'guess what I'm thinking,' and then inevitably finds the response lacking." Typically faculty members conduct classroom discussions by whipsawing students among plausible but conflicting rules for resolving the disputes which are at issue in the cases. Duncan Kennedy (1982: 45–46) has captured the students' frustration with characteristic panache as "trying to comprehend before a large audience a mind determined to elude you."

There seem to be two distinct but related explanations for this hit-and-miss approach to learning. Goodrich (1991: 101) makes sense of law school's bewildering pedagogy by concluding that "our professors *wanted* us to get lost in the legal wasteland, apparently, so we would treasure lawyerly skills when mastery finally came. I saw no other explanation: law school was intended to confuse, to intimidate, ultimately to indoctrinate."[8] Kennedy (1982: 47) makes a somewhat different point—explaining that the rules of the game are not divulged because, in effect, there are not, nor can there be, any such rules. He denies "legal reasoning is a distinct method for reaching correct results."

The upshot of all of this is, however, that students get two messages about lawyerly skills. On the one hand, they are led to believe that they will, that they *must*, learn to *think like lawyers* and that doing so is the secret of both academic achievement and a successful legal career. Indeed, they are led to believe that in learning to think like lawyers they are really learning to truly think for the first time in their lives. Learning to think like a lawyer is represented as abandoning the vagaries of lay thought and incorporating precision and agility into their cognitive processes.

The second message is that skillful and persuasive advocacy is dependent on political and moral agnosticism. Most students probably conclude their years in law school by believing that they emerge as both clear thinkers and effective advocates. At the outset of their legal education, however, many students sense instinctively a tension between mastering an elusive body of knowledge and developing rhetorical facility—and are deeply troubled. Goodrich (1991: 97) revealingly characterizes the resultant dilemma of the first-year law student: "Searching for elegance, I found only anarchy. But I couldn't surrender to anarchy, for that would kill something important in me—the belief that law had meaning beyond that manufactured in lawyers' heads. I still hoped to find a pattern, a reason to believe."

Legal education tends to breed, according to most commentators, an unsettling, pervasive, and corrosive skepticism among law students (Turow, 1977: 86):

"Legal thinking is nasty," I said to Gina at one point in our conversation, and I began later to think that I'd hit on a substantial truth. Thinking like a lawyer involved being suspicious and distrustful. You reevaluated statements inferred from silences, looked for loopholes and ambiguities. You did everything but take a statement at face value.

So on the one hand you believed nothing. And, on the other for the sake of logical consistency, and to preserve long-established rules, you would accept the most ridiculous fictions—that a corporation was a person, that an apartment tenant was renting land and not a dwelling.

Thinking in these terms tends to have a numbing impact on one's moral, political, and emotional sensibilities. Students may, at one and the same time, feel overwhelmed by the intellectual challenge of learning to think like a lawyer, captivated by their newly discovered analytical power, and (at least among the more reflective) mindful of an unwelcome personality change. "I felt addicted to law," Goodrich (1991: 115) confesses. "Law was so thrillingly empowering; how could I help but revel in its benefits."

Law students are left with little doubt about what it means to think like a lawyer and little doubt about what subverts legal thinking. Emotion and values are antithetical to legal thinking because they are represented as irredeemably subjective. Over and over again commentators note pressure on students to ignore issues of right and wrong and, accordingly, to repress any *feelings* that they might have about such matters. Kennedy (1982: 57–58), for example, detects a kind of law school version of the good cop–bad cop tactics—comprising *cold* cases followed by *hot* cases.

The first kind of case—call it a cold case— . . . can be on any subject, so long as it is of no political or moral or emotional significance. Just understand what happened and what's being said about it, you have to learn a lot of new terms, a little potted legal history, and lots of rules, none of which is carefully explained by the casebook or the teacher. . . . The other kind of case—call it a hot case—usually involves a sympathetic plaintiff—say, an Appalachian farm family—and an unsympathetic defendant—say a coal company. On first reading it appears that the coal company has screwed the farm family by renting their land for strip mining, with a promise to restore it to its original condition once the coal has been extracted, and then reneging on the promise. . . . The point of the class discussion will be that your initial reaction of outrage is naive, non-legal, irrelevant to what you're supposed to be learning, and may be substantively wrong in the bargain. There are "good reasons" for the awful result, when you take a legal and logical "large" view, as opposed to the knee-jerk passionate view; and if you can't muster those reasons, maybe you aren't cut out to be a lawyer.[9]

The alleged justifications for operating in moral-and-emotional neutral are both practical and principled. Judges will not take morality
and emotion seriously, and in any case, moral and emotional issues
generate ambiguity and sap rigor. Thus legal education sharpens the
mind by narrowing it—leaving out the very political and moral energy that fuels cause lawyering and inviting alienation as a condition
of work. As Goodrich puts it, "No doubt about it—two months of
law school had helped me speak better, analyze more deeply, think
more logically. But I had a nagging feeling that my outward appearance had become disconnected from my inner self, that my ability to
put a rational veneer on *anything* had made me a stranger to myself"
(Goodrich 1991: 105, italics added).

So far, we have focused almost exclusively on the cognitive elements of the retreat from cause lawyering during the course of legal
education. As described and analyzed in a substantial body of research, the cognitive transformation has a subliminal influence on
the cause lawyering impulse—an influence only dimly perceived by
most students. However, as we have already suggested and we will
now consider in more detail, there are also career-oriented messages,
which directly subvert the inclination to engage in cause lawyering.
While these two elements of legal education—"the ideology of pragmatism" (Granfield, 1992: 61) and the placement hierarchy to which
we now turn—are analytically distinct, they are inextricably embedded in legal education.

Legal Education, Legal Careers, and Cause Lawyering

Research on legal education suggests that most students begin ob-
sessing about careers right from the beginning, that they are encouraged to do so by the faculty, and that corporate law is represented as the central reward for academic success (Erlanger et al.,
1996). A common theme in student recollections of their first year is
how soon employment issues impinge on their law school experience. Interview season comes early—say, sometime in October.

Whereas third-year students are actually looking for a job, second- and first-year students are looking for summer internships which could, particularly for the second-years, be parlayed into full-time positions.

Irrespective of one's initial objectives, the contagious fixation on career issues seems virtually irresistible. Goodrich (1991: 131) reports that at Yale some students sign up for so many interviews that they "end up all but skipping classes in October." Clearly, at this point energy shifts from the pursuit of cognitive mastery to the pursuit of the material rewards. From one perspective, this autumnal frenzy is only a brief interlude. From another, its effects are more pervasive, and from the point of view of cause lawyering more pernicious. Even first-year students, for whom the immediate stakes of interview season are the lowest, develop a sudden but enduring awareness of both the centrality and the hierarchy of placement practices in legal education.

All of this comes as both a substantial shock and a direct assault on the initial inclinations of many of the students who are interested in cause lawyering. Turow's (1977: 91) first-year protagonist gets the message from an upperclassman: "The atmosphere is really something. . . . People go bananas about ZYX firm and XYZ firm. All this pressure begins to mount to take *any* job supposedly 'better' than another. You feel as though if you don't take the 'better' jobs then you're blowing all of the advantages built up by going to Harvard Law School." While the criteria for defining the "better job" are somewhat amorphous, they clearly seem to exclude the kinds of opportunities associated with cause lawyering. Instead, a better job is one with "bigger-named clients, salaries that are a little higher. If it's a government agency, the amount of power it wields and how much you'll have when you get there" (Turow, 1977: 91).

It also seems that large firms are disproportionately represented during interview season. Goodrich (1991: 128) reports that during the three weeks of "Job Fair" at Yale in 1986, "424 law firms and twenty-four government and public interest groups had signed up to interview second- and third-years at New Haven's downtown

Park Plaza Hotel." In addition, the big firms have more to offer the students—and do so early and often with considerable style. Kahlenberg (1992: 153) reports on his post–second year summer position with a prestigious Boston firm:

> As the summer at Ropes & Gray progressed, there were lunches and outings. There was the Labor Law Lunch, where the firm's lawyers discussed ways to counter various worker claims. . . . There was the firm outing . . . held at the Essex Club—a day filled with golf and tennis and filet mignon and speeches. There was the Corporate Lunch at the Meridien . . . where I learned that women at Ropes do trusts and estates and health care but not corporate law. There was the outing to see Mats Wilander and Andre Agassi play at the Longwood Tennis Club, where I spent much of the evening talking with a summer associate's boyfriend about leftist deconstructionist theory.

Kahlenberg (1992: 37) also offers a very clear picture of how and why corporate and private employment opportunities tend to trump both cause lawyering and public service jobs. Consider, to begin with, the discouraging results of his efforts as a first-year student to secure summer work as a cause lawyer. "The day after Thanksgiving, I sent out fifty-three letters to public-interest groups in New York, Washington and Boston. . . . But nearly a month after sending out resumes, I became depressed. Most places didn't respond at all. Of those that did, some said they hired only 2Ls and 3Ls; some said that they would not hire until March; others that they would take only volunteers."

Even more telling were the placement activities during Kahlenberg's third year. His job search went forward on two fronts—corporate and public service. With respect to the former, Kahlenberg was interviewed by and received offers from some of the leading firms in the country—including the prestigious Washington firms of Arnold & Porter and Covington & Burling. In the meantime, he was making virtually no headway on the other track: "In a wild failure of capitalism," he says, "I was faring much better with $70,000 law firm jobs than the $30,000 jobs on the Hill" (Kahlenberg, 1992: 190). Moreover, whereas the corporate firms had sought him out, his public service job search was conducted solely on his initiative and at his expense. If corporate careers are available on an assembly line, the path to cause lawyering is an obstacle course.

The most significant socializing force at work in law school turns out to be the social stratification, and prestige hierarchy, of the bar. Corporate practice sits atop the stratification and prestige hierarchy; everything else pales by comparison. The cognitive core of legal education, with its emphasis on the mastery of technical skills and the bracketing of moral commitment, prepares the way for students to succumb to the allure of the corporate law firm. The most important message that students are exposed to is to go where the money is. And, that is where most end up wanting to go.[10]

Sustaining Commitment

If the path to a cause lawyering career is an obstacle course, one might logically ask how is the persistence of some students to be explained? Why does a small coterie stick with cause or public service lawyering? Two elements seem to play a key role in answering this question. The first has to do with how those who are able to sustain their commitment to cause lawyering differed from the other incoming students, and the second has to do with what was special about their experiences while in law school.

With respect to the first dimension, Granfield's (1992) research is quite persuasive, if somewhat counterintuitive. His starting premise is that "law students are not simply empty vessels into which knowledge and consciousness is poured. Rather, they react to, struggle with, and interpret law" (Granfield, 1992: 52). Given this active engagement in the process, it stands to reason that what students bring with them to the socializing experience of legal education will influence what they take from it. Generally, one would assume that it is their idealism about law that sustains students in their commitment to cause lawyering.

Yet Granfield (1992) points us toward the cynics, not the idealists. Students seem better able to sustain a commitment to cause lawyering if they locate their political commitments outside law and come to law school with "no illusions about finding any abstract sense of justice in the law . . . [recognizing] that law maintains a system of structural injustice and inequality prevalent in capitalist society" (Granfield, 1992: 66–67).

Those who successfully resist the corrosive effects of law school on cause lawyering aspirations combine cynicism about law with an intense personal idealism—rooted in religious or spiritual commitments. They regard law as a "tool." The metaphor of law as a tool— as an instrument to be used, as one student stated, "against the law's normal inclinations" (Granfield, 1992: 69)—protected these students. They were more or less immune from the disabling disappointment that law school produces in those who come thinking of law in more idealized terms. Initial wariness about law protected them both from unrealistic expectations about what they could accomplish by way of cause lawyering and from disillusionment with the frailties of law and legality.

Association with other like-minded students also abetted sustaining commitment. Collective resistance was more effective as an "oppositional strategy" (Granfield, 1992: 69) than trying to go it alone. At Harvard, and at other law schools, collective resistance to the socialization process formed around institutionalized sources of opposition such as "the Labor Law Project, Students for Public Interest Law, Prisoner's Legal Assistance Project and the Legal Services Center. Some of these students even formed unofficial organizations such as 'The Counter-Hegemonic Front'" (Granfield, 1992: 69).

Stover (1989), reporting on his research at Denver, calls attention in particular to the National Lawyers Guild chapter as a focal point of effective resistance—as has other cause lawyering research (Scheingold, 1998). But he points to a variety of other subcultures of resistance, including "the American Civil Liberties Union, Women in Crisis, the conservative Mountain States Legal Foundation, the Native American Center of the Cheyenne and Arapaho Tribe," and so on (Stover, 1989: 109). Stover (1989: 109) concludes that these subcultures provided

- "support for the norm of professional altruism"
- "an image of public interest practice sharply at odds with the prevailing image of public interest ineptitude and marginality"
- "altruistically oriented students with the assurance that they . . . belonged to a broader community of like-minded persons"
- "role models"
- "a political point of view that heightened their commitment to public interest goals"

It is important to note that much of the resilience of the culture of resistance seems to come from its linkage to the world of legal practice (Wizner, 2001, 2002). By, for example, providing summer internships that are neither in private practice nor in government service, these institutionalized voices of cause lawyering offer a lifeline to the world outside the hermetically sealed ethos of legal education.

Paradoxically, then, it seems that it is those with grand visions of what law and lawyers should and can do on behalf of social justice who are most likely to abandon cause lawyering—while those with less lofty aspirations are more likely to stay the course. Put another way, these latter students arrive in law schools with a kind of built-in insulation against the disillusionment that students experience in law school. Nurtured by a subculture and associations that connect them to like-minded others, their idealism is insulated while they learn how strategically to deploy it to serve their cause lawyering aspirations.

Conclusion

In the opening chapters of this book we have been exploring the ways in which, to paraphrase Winston Churchill's celebrated observation, cause and conventional lawyers are divided by membership in a single profession. The resultant tensions drive cause lawyers to, but seldom beyond, the profession's boundaries. As we have already argued, the organized legal profession has made a place for cause lawyering—albeit a conditional and precarious place. Cause lawyering is tolerated, not encouraged, embraced when political conditions imperil the organized bar's legitimacy, but then stigmatized and marginalized when the threat abates.

This chapter has told an analogous tale about the plight of cause lawyering in the legal academy. Insofar as cause lawyering has a place in legal education and insofar as cause lawyering career aspirations persist through legal education, it is in spite of, not because of, the curriculum and the pedagogy of law schools. The marginalization of cause lawyering within the legal academy, as within the organized profession, is rooted in understandings of the centrality of disinterested client service to the definition of lawyer professionalism. Administrators, faculty, and most students experience the expectations and values of would-be cause lawyers as threats to the status, the integrity, and the mission of the profession and of the role of legal education in serving the profession.

As in the profession at large, the extracurricular projects that nurture cause lawyering in law school are associated with doing good and, thus, provide law schools with a modicum of public service credibility—and do so without impinging on their vocational mission. Indeed, because many of these projects offer practical experience, they supplement clinical programs and partially compensate for the deficiencies that critics detect in the largely theoretical curricula of the major law schools. Accordingly, cause lawyering survives largely within a tolerated extracurricular subculture. It is at once valorized in the hortatory rhetoric that seeks to explain what legal education contributes to society and yet marginalized in the day-to-day practices of law schools.[11]

What is true of the organized profession and legal education is equally true of legal practice. We will discover in the chapters that follow that idealism may or may not be a necessary condition of cause lawyering, but it is certainly not a sufficient condition. For cause lawyers, legal practice is replete with the same kinds of obstacles that they faced in law school. Just as in law school, these obstacles both take their toll on and provide inspiration for the practice of cause lawyering. After all, the distinctive social and professional contributions of cause lawyering flow directly from, and are made possible by, the structural contestations between it and the legal academy, the bar, and the bench. For some, the rewards of cause lawyering are insufficient and its burdens too heavy. Others thrive, or at least persevere, because of who they are and where they work, and because of the prevailing political and social ethos.

CHAPTER 4

Careers in Cause Lawyering: Risks and Rewards

> The complex relations between cause lawyering and the legal profession and the delicate negotiation required by those who seek to do political work within the practice of law are not simply abstract theoretical issues. They are played out in the day-to-day work that cause lawyers do, in the way they organize their practices, in their relations with clients, and in the strategic decisions they make.
>
> Sarat and Scheingold, 1998b

IN THIS CHAPTER we move from considering the principles of, and the preparation for, cause lawyering to cause lawyering in action. We consider the varied meanings of cause lawyering that are constituted in and through the work cause lawyers do. We examine the risks and rewards of cause lawyering and, in particular, how cause lawyering careers are shaped by conditions at the practice site. The practice site is an essential locus for working out the tensions that are always a part of the cause lawyering enterprise. As Robert Nelson and David Trubek (1992b: 205) put it, "The legal workplace is an arena of professionalism in the sense that the specific organizational contexts in which lawyers work produce and reflect particular visions of professional ideals."

In the next chapter, we will explore cause lawyering as a democratic political project. While analytically separable, these two elements of cause lawyering in action are inextricably interdependent. Where one practices influences how one practices, whether one can push beyond conventional types of lawyering work to politicize practice, what one can accomplish, and—when considered in the aggregate—the capacity of cause lawyering to contribute to democracy.

So far, our central claim has been that cause lawyering arises out of a search by attorneys to unify profession and belief—an effort, that is, to escape the constraints of the ideology of advocacy (Simon, 1978; Luban, 1988) and to maximize the consonance between moral values and professional practice. In this chapter, as we examine cause lawyering in practice, we complicate this identification of cause lawyering with an unalienated and unalienating professional life (Spaulding, 2003). Cause lawyering is, after all, a vocation in which people pursue their version of a more just society while they work to make a living. Put simply, only insofar as it provides a materially adequate, as well as a morally fulfilling, way of life is a career in cause lawyering feasible. Cause lawyers may or may not be altruists (Menkel-Meadow, 1998), but without economic sustenance they cannot survive as lawyers.

Whether, how, and to what extent a personally satisfying mix of values and interests can be constructed depends on conditions at the practice site and on how those conditions fit with the broader political ethos.[1] In this chapter we examine three sites in which cause lawyering is situated: pro bono programs in corporate firms, salaried practice in public and private agencies, and small firms.[2] Each of the three offers a distinctive pattern of risk and reward and, consequently, its own career path.

Our objective is neither to identify an ideal workplace nor to rank them. This is in part because the patterns of risk and reward at the practice site change through time. In addition, what constitutes an acceptable balance of political commitment and material reward varies among cause lawyers. Briefly put, therefore, we want to provide an account of how practice site interacts with personal beliefs and political conditions to shape cause lawyering work.[3] Because there simply is no perfect site, nor stable and certain patterns of risk and reward associated with particular workplaces, our focus will be on career *possibilities* at each practice site and on the factors which explain variation from site to site and time to time.

Corporate Cause Lawyering

At first glance it might seem that attorneys with cause lawyering aspirations would and should steer clear of corporate practice (Granfield and Koenig, 2003). Corporate practice, by definition, does not provide a venue for full-time devotion to a cause. Much of corporate practice requires just the kind of marginalization of commitment and belief that cause lawyers eschew (Kagan and Rosen, 1985). And except for right-wing cause lawyers, working in corporate firms might well seem rather like sleeping with the enemy.

Nonetheless, corporate firms' pro bono programs provide a potentially important venue for cause lawyering, a venue in which lawyers are able to devote at least a small portion of their professional lives to causes in which they believe (Rhode, 2000b). They are able to do so by deploying the substantial resources of corporate law firms on behalf of those causes. And, for many causes—for example, the movement to abolish the death penalty or the environmental movement—the contribution of corporate pro bono programs is quite significant (Davis, 2001).

While they provide lawyers and resources which many causes sorely need (Wernz, 2002), those programs also serve to legitimate the firms themselves, taking the hard edge off an image of lawyers serving, uncritically, the needs and interests of capital (Maute, 2002). In addition, despite the beating that cause lawyering takes in law school, some of the best and the brightest do themselves come out of law school with their ideals intact or with a sense of an ethical responsibility to give something back. Thus, pro bono programs tend to enhance the attraction of corporate firms to some newly minted lawyers while at the same time embellishing the reputation of corporate lawyers as contributors to civic well-being.

More broadly, as we have noted earlier, pro bono programs are seen as intrinsic to the ethical responsibilities of the legal profession as a whole (Carle, 2001). Thus, it should come as no surprise that, as Scott Cummings (2004) has documented, the ABA has been instrumental in the widespread institutionalization of pro bono programs in large corporate firms. This institutionalization has given impetus to the transformation of pro bono responsibilities from a hortatory admonition into an operative ethical injunction.

Pro bono programs are, as Cummings (2004: 29) emphasizes, now "the lynchpin of an increasingly privatized system of public interest advocacy." In other words, instead of being responsive to the causes that inspired the volunteer attorneys, pro bono is entirely driven by the needs of the firm. The research findings that we will present below—dealing primarily with the pro bono practices of individual corporate firms—are entirely consistent with Cummings's (2004: 100) skepticism about institutionalization—namely, that "anchoring poverty legal services in the restrictive environment of the large firm has the effect of circumscribing the space for transgressive practice." (On transgressive cause lawyering, see Scheingold and Bloom, 1998.)

Even in the most public-spirited corporate firms, we will argue, there is never any doubt that pro bono programs are welcome only insofar as, and to the extent that, they do not interfere with serving corporate clients and with providing a more than comfortable income for the partners (Epstein, 2002). We will explore how cause lawyering, as defined in Chapter 1, can collide with a firm's capacity to enhance its social and financial capital. We will also consider the numerous ways in which pro bono programs have been designed to minimize such risks—often at the cost of real opportunities for cause lawyering. Finally, even with institutionalization, the commitment of firms to pro bono is modest at best. As Deborah Rhode (2000b: 37) puts it, "Involvement in public interest and poverty law programs remains minimal at many of the nation's leading law firms." In sum,

the institutionalization of pro bono programs reported by Cummings is one element of the domestication of cause lawyering.

Pro Bono Programs: Theme and Variation

Corporate law firms may be gracious or grudging in how they finance pro bono programs, as well as programmatically expansive or
restrictive. The major issue is the extent to which firm resources are
made available for pro bono activities. As Michael Kelly (1994: 2–3)
and others have noted, today the "culture of practice" is being transformed by the pervasive emergence of "larger and stronger" organizations that are more economically self-conscious and are responding to the financial or budgetary goals of their ownership. According
to Kelly's (1994) research, limiting pro bono programs is one of the
results of this transformation of law firm culture.

The most obvious indicator of a firm's willingness to commit resources to pro bono lawyering is the way billable hours are handled.
When billable-hours requirements expand, as they have in recent
years, the amount of time that can be devoted to pro bono work declines (Fortney, 2003; Richmond, 2002). Still, billable-hours requirements and pro bono programs need not become a zero-sum game.
The tension between them can be alleviated insofar as billable-hours
requirements are adjusted to compensate for pro bono work.

Assume, for example, that associates are expected to bill two
thousand hours. Are attorneys given full or at least partial credit for
their pro bono work? Or are they simply encouraged to do pro bono
work off the clock? Similarly, what allowance, if any, is made for the
occasional big case that eats up hours and support services? Having
rigidly construed rules concerning time and money spent on pro
bono lawyering means that attorneys will be able to engage only
ephemerally with causes (Fortney, 2003). Serious engagement im-
plies a willingness to tackle big cases that can be time-consuming
and unpredictable.[4]

There are also more subtle ways of neutering pro bono programs
(Granfield and Koenig, 2003). Putting an associate instead of a

prominent partner in charge of the program conveys an unmistakable message to young associates who do the lion's share of pro bono lawyering in corporate firms. Another indication of a lukewarm commitment to pro bono is its conflation with firm development— for example, by treating free service to prominent civic organizations as pro bono work. In many firms pro bono work "goes . . . to family, friends, clients who fail to pay their fees, and middle-class organizations like hospitals and schools that might become paying clients" (Rhode, 2000b: 37). Mixing with the civic elite is a time-tested way of making contacts that can generate clients while at the same time embellishing the reputation of the firm with those who count in the community. When this signal is accompanied by the message that even beginning associates have firm-development responsibilities, the handwriting is on the wall. The result is to discourage associates from responding even to unmet legal needs—not to mention broader cause lawyering goals (Rhode, 1999).

The interpretation of conflict-of-interest rules also has direct implications for the cause lawyering opportunities available in corporate practice. Of course, direct conflicts of interest are prohibited for both pro bono and fee-for-service clients. So-called *positional* conflicts are another matter, but the line between them can blur (Shapiro, 2003). Conflicts are direct insofar as a pro bono client is engaged in an adversary relationship with one of the firm's regular clients. Positional conflicts occur when the pro bono client is pursuing an objective that runs counter to the perceived interests of one or more of the firm's clients. Take, for example, an attorney who wishes to pursue environmental causes but whose firm represents timber, natural gas, oil, or coal interests (Lardent, 1999). Still more restrictively interpreted, positional conflicts are perceived in pro bono activities that might merely *offend* the firm's regular clients or its prospective clients. Suffice it to say that conflict-of-interest issues are endemic to cause lawyering in corporate practice because corporate mischief is often the target of cause lawyering (Shamir, forthcoming).

From a broader perspective, it is important to recognize that what is permissible in corporate pro bono programs is really as much about working within the boundaries of civic respectability as it is about conflicts of interest or even politics. Consider the example of two Seattle attorneys. One was not permitted to represent the Northwest Women's Law Center in a case against Operation Rescue. The other was only reluctantly allowed to represent a gay military officer in a discharge case (Scheingold and Bloom, 1998: 224). Similarly, a Christian cause lawyer found himself estranged from corporate practice by his partners who "viewed him as 'one of those wild-eyed evangelicals.'" One of these partners complained that "the religious right . . . makes my flesh crawl." Conversely, the Christian cause lawyer thought of his partners as "worshiping 'two false gods—personal autonomy and wealth'" (Heinz, Paik, and Southworth, 2003: 40). The message to young associates is to steer clear of controversial causes—whether on the left or on the right.

Accommodating Personal Aspirations to Corporate Practice

As the foregoing indicates, accommodations are a fact of life in corporate firms. How associates respond to the opportunities and constraints of corporate pro bono programs varies according to personality, commitment to cause lawyering, and firm culture. Accommodation to constraints in pro bono programs is a reliable indicator of who is and who is not serious about cause lawyering. In short, patterns of accommodation further help locate the boundary between conventional and cause lawyering.

Some associates welcome meagerly funded or narrowly conceived pro bono programs. Insofar as a lawyer's aspirations are confined to making a modest contribution to unmet legal needs, recent changes in the circumstances of corporate practice will probably seem a step in the right direction (Fortney, 2003). For a lawyer who thinks primarily in terms of an ethical responsibility to engage in pro bono activities, a limited program provides an opportunity to remain on the fast track while doing a bit of good. For others, the shift of resources away from pro bono programs and the increased emphasis on firm development may even be a kind of blessing in disguise. While they feel they *should* be doing pro bono work, they don't find this work particularly rewarding. Indeed, some corporate attorneys find that working for people at the margins can be very frustrating. As one attorney put it, the work is often without "intellectual challenge," the clients themselves "are just totally irresponsible," and there is "rarely a clear victory" (Scheingold and Bloom, 1998: 227).

Conversely, lawyers who are deeply committed to cause lawyering, even within the context of a corporate practice, view a retreat from pro bono programs with alarm. They approach their pro bono work as a cherished break from the routines of corporate practice as well an opportunity to do good.[5] Cause lawyering is, especially for young associates, distinctly preferable to the minutiae involved in doing big cases for large, impersonal institutions. Unlike the reluctant pro bono practitioner, would-be cause lawyers may welcome the humanizing impact of intense engagement with marginalized clients—like those on death row. One associate in a large firm put it this way: "I like having personal involvement in my work and feeling like the work that I do has a personal impact on people's lives, which I somehow don't feel when I'm writing briefs for [names a corporation]" (Scheingold and Bloom, 1998: 227).

As for doing good, it might seem that conflict-of-interest issues can be readily dealt with by shifting away from favored but controversial causes like abortion rights, defense of gays and lesbians, or protection of the spotted owl. After all, there is no shortage of causes in which to believe. However, a dedicated lawyer who is committed to a particular cause or is working for a restrictive firm can be put in an awkward situation, and as a result some corporate attorneys end up trimming their cause lawyering sails (Wernz, 2002). Another option is to do one's controversial cause lawyering off the books—on one's own time with one's own resources or those of an advocacy organization like the American Civil Liberties Union.

Insofar as a life of constant accommodation is unacceptable, the only option is to exit corporate practice. While that does indeed happen, exit is far and away the exception rather than the rule. By and large, attorneys gravitate toward corporate firms because they see the compromises as acceptable and outweighed by the benefits of corporate practice. Corporate pro bono provides a way of *doing* cause lawyering without *being* a cause lawyer.

Given the context—one in which firms jealously guard their public reputations—cause lawyering in corporate firms is constrained and moderated. Consider, after all, the modest amount of time that can be devoted to it; the extent to which one's priority interests may be off the table; and, of course, the fact that most of one's time must be devoted to commodified practice on behalf of corporate interests. Yet pro bono permits episodic, though often highly consequential, involvement with social movements for lawyers whose day-to-day work is client-oriented. It provides islands of time in which agnosticism can be displaced, at least temporarily, by conviction.

Salaried Cause Lawyering

The classic sites for cause lawyers to practice are public agencies, like the legal services program and privately funded advocacy organizations such as the Manhattan Institute. Here the practice setting allows full-time advocacy for a cause. Nor is there any need to worry about sleeping with the enemy. By choosing organizations that are committed to causes in which they believe, salaried lawyers escape in one fell swoop the tyranny of the ideology of advocacy, the vicissitudes of the market for legal services, and the pressure to increase billable hours to levels that put one's physical and emotional health at risk.[6]

On the other hand, they receive much more modest remuneration than what is provided in corporate firms. Ann Southworth (forthcoming: 13) reports that on the right "several lawyers for religious organizations worked in extremely modest circumstances, and one lawyer active on abortion and religious liberties issues asserted that he and another respondent were the lowest paid members of their" elite law school class. While there are no systematic data available, it stands to reason that compensation varies among sites of salaried practice. For example, Southworth (forthcoming: 13) suspects that lawyers for libertarian organizations tend to be better paid than those who work for the religious right. Still, modest to moderate levels of compensation emerge as a constant of this kind of cause lawyering practice.

There are, however, telling variations in the risks and rewards available *among* sites of salaried practice. In some organizations it is possible to have a secure position, civilized working conditions, *and* the opportunity to vigorously pursue one's political objectives. In other organizations, or at other times, salaried practice can be much more confining, lacking the opportunity to take on high-stakes impact litigation or to engage in overtly political action. In short, while salaried cause lawyering allows lawyers to be consistently on the "right" side, what one can reasonably hope to accomplish varies from time to time and place to place—with that variation driven largely by the preferences and priorities of the agencies that fund the work.

Aspirations, Constraints, and Strategic Options

One of the most well-known sites of cause lawyering is the National Association for the Advancement of Colored People (NAACP), which led the struggle against desegregation (Carle, 2002). The NAACP, like many other organizations of the liberal left, has been unequivocally committed to the use of litigation as a vehicle of social change because of the abiding belief of its founders in the law-politics distinction (Kluger, 1977). Accordingly, the NAACP resisted efforts of other civil rights organizations to engage in political protest against "massive resistance" to *Brown v. Board of Education* and other NAACP courtroom victories. This cautious approach put the NAACP at odds with more aggressive elements of the civil rights movement, which organized freedom rides, street protests, boycotts, and other kinds of direct action (Kluger, 1977). In these latter organizations, lawyers were largely relegated to legal defense work on behalf of the activists who spearheaded the movement.

In other advocacy organizations lawyers often feel burdened by the constraints of law. One example is provided by the rise and fall of the Office of Economic Opportunity's Legal Services Program. This government-funded legal arm of the War on Poverty had a schizophrenic mandate. Its most ambitious proponents believed that it was possible to wage direct and effective legal warfare on poverty (Cahn and Cahn, 1964). At the same time, Legal Services was charged with providing symptomatic relief for impecunious clients who could not afford legal representation in the mundane struggles of daily life—domestic relations disputes concerning divorce and child custody, landlord-tenant controversies, and the like. Predictably, while client representation has proved largely unremarkable, more enterprising strategies directed at the sources of poverty proved more controversial (Feldman, 1985).[7]

Indeed, there is, as we noted in Chapter 2, no more sobering example of the perils of politicization than the legal services program—and in particular the California Rural Legal Assistance Program (CRLA). Its success in combining litigation and political action to help organize nonunionized and notoriously exploited migrant agricultural workers in California made clear that legal services could make meaningful structural contributions to the War on Poverty. The reaction of California's powerful agricultural lobby was predictable and resulted in long-term, and largely successful, efforts to bring both the CRLA and the legal services program itself to heel.

For a while, after the political climate became more conservative and more hostile, resourceful program directors were able to devise strategies that took some of the sting out of national directives. That is, however, no longer the case. Funding has been dramatically reduced, program governance has been increasingly put in the hands of conservative appointees, and the program is no longer schizophrenic because virtually the only responsibility remaining for legal services attorneys is client representation—dealing, that is, solely with poverty's symptoms (see Luban, 2003).

While the experiences of the legal services program are especially dramatic, the underlying choices are much the same in most sites of salaried practice. During the period that legal services programs were shrinking in size and in aspiration, public defender programs tended to flourish. Still, criminal defense work mostly comprises what public defenders tend to see as an endless and largely futile struggle on behalf of individual clients—many of whom could reasonably be thought of as victims of an implacably punitive state and a profoundly discriminatory criminal justice system (Tonry, 1995).

The only relief available from this treadmill is appellate work, which rescues public defenders from the daily grind of crushing caseloads and provides an opportunity to correct illicit legal and constitutional practices. Note, however, that even at its appellate best, public defender work is strictly about law. As a result, public defenders are sheltered from the kind of reprisals suffered by the legal services program. The cost is that their kind of cause lawyering is much less political and largely cut off from social movements with political agendas.

It is not, however, only publicly funded cause lawyers who experience such constraints and dilemmas. Occasionally privately funded, salaried cause lawyering is limited largely to noncontroversial litigation. Practically speaking, organizations funded by civic elites tend to be very careful not to rock the boat. Cause lawyers in these settings ordinarily confine themselves to relatively apolitical goals and tactics (Scheingold and Bloom, 1998). Laura Hatcher (forthcoming) finds much the same constraints among organizations funding right-wing cause lawyering. She notes that the Pacific Legal Foundation is committed to lobbying legislators, while the Institute for Justice pursues constitutional litigation. Thus both of these organizations confine themselves to means that are widely accepted within the professional and political mainstream.

There are, however, exceptions to this general rule—organizations in which salaried cause lawyers can engage in more overtly politicized legal practices. Labor unions can be such a site—at least for those who identify with the union movement. While it is true that union attorneys must face up to the constraints of limited funding and thus to not being able to pursue all legitimate workplace grievances, they are also aware that association with the union means working at a site of institutionalized political and social action.

Michael McCann's (1994) research on the pay equity movement reveals how attorneys working together with union organizers were able to parlay litigation (even losing litigation) into consciousness-raising and movement-building activities among women workers. As he puts it (1994: 279–80), the pay equity movement's claim of "equal pay for work of comparable worth derived in large part from previous battles" was effectively deployed "to raise the expectations and channel the energies of working women already well aware of their unfair treatment." In sum, unions provide one stable and focused practice site where legal work can reasonably be seen as part of a broader struggle. Thus, whereas both poverty lawyers and public defenders have largely been reduced to administering legal first aid to the victims of an increasingly harsh political climate, union lawyers can reasonably see their defense of victims in the broader context of affirmative political strategies.

Similarly, Susan Coutin found that immigration reform lawyers working for Central American community organizations funded during the 1980s to support democratic political movements in their home countries engaged in a highly politicized form of legal practice.

This work required cause lawyers to participate in broad-based movements that sought justice for Central American immigrants. These movements were transnational in character, drew on both official and clandestine networks, and promoted multiple models of statehood, membership, and legitimacy. Attorneys sometimes participated in these movements directly. In addition, as members of organizations that were involved in political advocacy, attorneys were implicitly supporting this work. (Coutin 2001: 133)

In short, Coutin's (2001: 132) account of immigration cause lawyers reveals robust political advocacy which "was not limited to helping immigrants discover ways to manipulate U.S. immigration law and thus to win in court."

Recently, *The New Yorker* (Bowe, 2003: 121) provided an account of a successful campaign against "slave labor" practices in Florida. Reminiscent of the CRLA efforts in California in the 1960s, the Florida campaign was spearheaded by the Coalition of Immokalee Workers (CIW)—a community organization with "more than two thousand members." The CIW was created in the 1990s with the help of two Florida Legal Services attorneys. Its focus was on mobilizing field-workers and included clandestine activities which led to "uncovering and investigating abusive employers, locating transient witnesses, and encouraging them to overcome their fears of testifying against their former captors."

These efforts produced evidence which persuaded a reluctant Justice Department to prosecute and convict two brothers who had, in effect, created a system of "modern slavery" which was built in equal parts on peonage and terror. Once again, as with McCann's (1994) and Coutin's (2001) findings, overtly politicized cause lawyering is made possible when lawyers are funded by organizations which are themselves driven by political goals and are not dependent on mainstream funding sources.[8]

*Accommodating Personal Aspirations
to Salaried Practice*

There is at least one sense in which cause lawyers in salaried practice are prototypical *cause* lawyers. Organizational missions tend to be relatively clear-cut, and an attorney signing on with an organization can generally speaking have a much better idea of the cause to be served than either the corporate cause lawyers discussed above or the small-firm cause lawyers to be considered next. Yet sometimes the attractions of salaried practice are diminished by timid tactics or by an equivocal organizational mandate. Even then, however, there are secondary rewards which make salaried practice more appealing for some cause lawyers than either corporate or small-firm practice, despite the financial rewards of the former and enhanced freedom of the latter.

To begin with, the organizational mission is often crystal clear and is pursued vigorously. Consider what Southworth (forthcoming; see also Heinz, Paik, and Southworth, 2003: 40) found among cause lawyers employed by advocacy organizations of the Christian right:

Three Christian evangelical lawyers who had left private practice to work full-time for religious advocacy groups described their decisions in religious terms. One said: "The idols in my life were money and prestige and people being proud of me and having a fancy job and making money. And I had always heard in church the claims that God makes about himself and that he is worthy of worship and devotion of one's life to him and started thinking: 'Maybe you're supposed to take that seriously.'" Another recounted how becoming a born-again Christian led him to conclude that "This change in my life, acknowledging, recognizing that I'm a Christian, should have something to do with how I spend the better part of my day, what my job is, what my career is, what my vocation is, what my calling is."[9]

However, salaried cause lawyers regularly confront much less comfortable circumstances. For example, cause lawyers in public defense work can believe that they are doing political work in that they are "fighting the state." Yet these attorneys are well aware that they are providing only Band-Aid relief. As one politically committed public defender put it, "Like being a social worker, like trying to run a shelter. I don't consider it part of a real attempt at forming political change, structural change, the kind that we eventually need" (Scheingold and Bloom, 1998: 235). And what of feminist criminal defense lawyers who are asked to represent someone charged with sexual violence, for example? For them, cause lawyering may feel uncomfortably close to the ideology of advocacy. In short, salaried practitioners often have to accommodate organizational means and ends which run counter to their own.

Still, there are a variety of things that make salaried practice attractive even in problematic situations. If one is not entirely or aggressively on the right side, at least one is unlikely to be on the wrong side (Sarat, 1998a). From this perspective, salaried practice for moderately reformist advocacy organizations is an appealing alternative to pro bono corporate cause lawyering. Take, for example, an attorney who went to work for Seattle's Northwest Women's Law

Center (NWLC). She saw feminist issues as congenial to her sensibilities but hardly as her vocation. She acknowledged that until the NWLC opportunity came along, she was prepared to go in-house for a corporation on the assumption that she could use her insider position to work against employment discrimination, sexual harassment, and the like. In other words, her aspirations were largely indistinguishable from those of corporate cause lawyers, but working full-time on women's issues seemed like a step in the right direction.

Even for more politically committed cause lawyers, one of the strong appeals of salaried practice is the opportunity it provides to escape the burdens of commodified legal services. The oppressive tyranny of billable hours weighs heavily on those who see salaried practice as the preferred cause lawyering alternative. Consider what the politically committed public defender cited above had to say:

Why am I not doing private practice? Probably the biggest reason is, if I want to run a small business I could have stayed in Chicago and been a wedding photographer like my father, my grandfather, my brother. I'm serious about that. I grew up in a family of small businessmen. I've chosen something else in part because I'm not very good at the business sense, and I have absolutely no desire to run my own office, to build clients, to pay support staff. I prefer to have a regular income and not have to worry about business details. (Scheingold and Bloom, 1998: 231)

This response provides only a glimpse of what salaried practitioners find objectionable in private practice. "The worst thing about private practice was that I thought about money every single day. . . . There's an interesting tension when you get into thinking about what people are paying you, you also inevitably think about how much work you should do on their case. . . . So I was constantly dealing with that tension. And I found that I didn't like the sort of ways I was thinking about things where how much more should I do was always on my mind" (Scheingold and Bloom, 1998: 231). Fee-for-service lawyering can, in other words, take a pervasive moral and emotional toll. Many cause lawyers simply find it very difficult to reconcile their beliefs with their profession when they are forced to deliver legal services as a commodity. Accordingly, salaried practice provides a refuge from the burdens of the business side of legal services.

Finally and paradoxically, salaried practice, even in cautiously mainstream advocacy organizations, can have a particular appeal for the most politically engaged cause lawyers. Unlike corporate or small-firm practice, salaried attorneys find it relatively easy to distinguish their own time from what is expected of them on the job. In addition, their regular salaries allow them to pursue their more explicitly political activity—advising, participating in, or defending grassroots social movements. As one lawyer put it, "I still believe that doing direct action—blockading the street, building a wall around the consulate, blockading Operation Rescue people to their own churchyard, all of which are things we've done—are useful in helping to build whatever movement that they relate to, if nothing else to raise morale within the group of people doing it, to feel like they're acting" (Scheingold and Bloom, 1998: 236).

Small-Firm Cause Lawyering

Personal autonomy is the major objective of cause lawyers who turn to small-firm practice[10]—freedom, that is, to pursue goals in which they believe, to work with colleagues with whom they feel comfortable, and to utilize whatever tactics they deem appropriate. Cause lawyers working in small firms tend to take on a diverse portfolio rather than devoting themselves, like those who work for advocacy organizations, to a single cause. Of course, their freedom to choose is constrained by the need to generate sufficient income to remain financially viable.

Small-firm practitioners have to combine politically satisfying work with the necessity to generate sufficient income to remain economically viable. They may be content to put conventional legal tactics at the service of well-established constitutional goals (Barclay and Marshall, forthcoming). On the other hand, small-firm practice is an especially congenial site for cause lawyers inclined to transgress the boundaries of political and professional respectability. Either way, small-firm practice provides a venue for like-minded cause lawyers to follow their muses.

To offer but one example, consider the impromptu mix of motives and objectives driving the small Detroit firm of Marks and Feinberg (see Kelly, 1994). The founding partners, as well as the attorneys that came on board subsequently, all had tried to pursue cause lawyering in other ways and in other settings. Feinberg himself began his career in a small firm which "represented a number of labor unions and specialized in low- and middle-income housing" (Kelly, 1994: 145). He left that firm because he "disliked his day-to-day diet of commercial litigation, tax law and estates and trusts" (Kelly, 1994: 145–46). The others came from salaried practice, and the new firm initially seemed less about a mission or a plan than about the opportunity to tailor a practice to each attorney's preferences and expertise.

Thirty-five to 40 percent of their work is criminal defense, mostly referrals from other community-based lawyers. Little of this is lucrative white-collar criminal-defense work. Perhaps as much as a third of the practice is devoted to employment discrimination, particularly in the area of academic employment problems, including revocation of professional licenses. In addition to miscellaneous civil rights cases, including prisoner rights, they have recently begun to handle some personal injury, medical malpractice and products liability work, but it is a comparatively small part of the practice compared to the employment and criminal matters. (Kelly, 1994: 146–47)

The firm did not fashion a grand scheme nor commit itself to a single cause. Instead, a diverse array of worthwhile causes was pursued. Taken together, these causes reflected a determination to use law for politically progressive purposes. At the same time, their diversity enabled the members of the firm to play to their own respective strengths and preferences.

While small-firm cause lawyering provides freedom of choice, it also puts the attorneys' social capital at risk. Small firms are in what is considered the lower hemisphere of legal practice—generally serving causes by representing individuals rather than institutions (Heinz and Laumann, 1982). In the status hierarchy of the legal profession, individual clients are viewed as second best because they have neither the deep pockets nor the intellectually complex and financially rewarding legal problems of institutional clients. Accordingly, small-firm cause lawyering usually means a modest income and suspect professional status.

Small-firm practitioners are, moreover, very much "in business," and ordinarily in a financially precarious business (Carlin, 1962; and Landon, 1990). Consider the severe financial pressures experienced by three Seattle small-firm cause lawyers. "We live on the bubble here," said one, "from paycheck to paycheck." Another mentioned the firm's "hard, hard times." A third reported a year in which he had earned "under $10,000" (Scheingold and Bloom, 1998: 241). In this sense, too, the constant struggle of the Marks and Feinberg firm to somehow make enough money to keep the practice afloat (Kelly, 1994) typifies small-firm cause lawyering. Taken together, the unwelcome necessity to commodify the delivery of legal services and the predominance of attorneys determined to do things their own way make small-firm practice more volatile than corporate and salaried cause lawyering.

Aspirations, Constraints, and Strategic Options

There was a time, however, in the late 1960s and early 1970s when the prospects for small-firm cause lawyering on the left seemed quite promising. To begin with, the market for legal services made it relatively easy to finance cause lawyering by way of paying clients whose goals would not put one's principles at risk. For example, a Seattle lawyer who practiced in a legal collective in the late 1960s and early 1970s put it this way: "I think it was legally a very fortunate time when we started our collective. It was really remarkably easy for us to get going and make a living. . . . It was a lot less competitive than it is now. . . . It's very much more difficult [now], I think, as a solo practitioner generalist to survive economically" (Scheingold and Bloom, 1998: 241).

In addition, the relatively congenial political context gave small-firm cause lawyers a sense of being part of an egalitarian, democratic political movement that was making meaningful progress. Simply put, small-firm cause lawyering nurtured autonomy and choice while at the same time imparting a sense of purposeful solidarity and accomplishment.

These days the political plight of small-firm cause lawyers on the left is diametrically different—particularly those who wish to engage politically. As one such lawyer put it, "The movement as it existed in the 1960s and 1970s doesn't exist any more. . . . So here I am out there still trying to do this legal stuff that's not linked to any movement, and so what's the point of what I'm doing? I have to go back and re-examine" (Scheingold and Bloom, 1998: 241).

On the right, in contrast, small firms look especially appealing to-day because they are, much like their counterparts on the left in an earlier era, sailing with the prevailing political winds. Thus, South-worth (forthcoming) reports that of the lawyers on the right that she interviewed, "eight of the lawyers who appeared to identify most strongly with the causes they served were in solo or small firm prac-tices in which they mixed paid and unpaid work. One of these lawyers indicated that he spends fifty percent of his professional time on uncompensated work, all of which dovetails with his com-mitment to 'faith-based' approaches to social problems." At the same time that small-firm cause lawyers on the left must cope with less re-warding political prospects, they must also deal with a much tighter market for legal services. It is not clear whether market conditions are equally problematic on the right.

There are a number of ways to fund small-firm practice—al-though on their face they seem disproportionately relevant to causes of the left rather than the right. Settlements are available from em-ployment discrimination litigation and from police misconduct cases. In addition, courts are permitted to award fees under federal civil rights statutes. The government also funds private attorneys ap-pointed to represent defendants in federal cases in general and in death penalty cases in particular.

Nonetheless, as we have already noted, the finances of most small firms tend to be precarious. The result is that financial considerations force small-firm practitioners to adjust downward the amount of cause-oriented litigation they do. This can mean simply taking on fewer or less financially risky cause lawyering cases. In addition, life cycle changes may well lead to altered priorities among the firm's membership. One Seattle small-firm attorney complained that "there are people here who want to essentially be rich and that's a tension. And if you're going to be rich, you have to do less risky and more sure thing litigation" (Scheingold and Bloom, 1998: 240).

Small-firm cause lawyers must, in short, struggle to maintain a satisfactory measure of cause lawyering while avoiding the temptation of paying clients who compromise the values driving the firm. Here, it is worth noting that cause lawyers in *solo* practice may find it easier to strike a satisfying balance. One small-firm lawyer who had been in solo practice summed it all up:

> It was somewhat easier [in my own firm] in that I wasn't answerable to anybody else and if I decided that I wanted to spend 20 or 30 hours in a given month and not get paid for it, I wasn't answerable to anybody. I just earned less. Here [in the small firm], it is a little bit more complex. In truth, nobody hassles me. . . . But there is a sense of other people kind of looking at the hours you work, the receipts that you bring in, and [you] want to feel that you are justifying the salary they are paying you. So in that sense there's a sense that it's not completely my own choice. (Scheingold and Bloom, 1998: 251)

In any event, the financial problems that plague small-firm cause lawyering enhance the importance of shared political commitment and compatibility among lawyers while making it more difficult to maintain them.

Persistence and Accommodation

Despite all of the problems that plague small-firm cause lawyering, it is likely to remain an important site for this work for two reasons. On the one hand, small-firm cause lawyering offers a unique combination of personal independence and collegial compatibility (Trubek and Kransberger, 1998). In addition, while small-firm practice is no bed of roses, enterprising and opportunistic practitioners have demonstrated that reasonably satisfactory accommodations can be worked out.

The opportunity to pursue one's priorities in the company of like-minded colleagues is a core appeal of small-firm cause lawyering. Thus, hiring in small cause lawyering firms necessarily incorporates a political or moral litmus test—whether defined broadly in terms of right and left or more narrowly in terms of a shared ideology, convergent or collective goals, and synchronous passions. The hiring practices of left-liberal firms are likely to be designed, as a partner in a Seattle civil liberties–oriented firm put it, to "weed out the right wingers . . . and the Republicans" (Scheingold and Bloom, 1998: 240). Especially in small firms with clear, ideologically pure missions, choosing colleagues and selecting causes are inextricably linked. This seems to be equally true among left-wing firms like Marks and Feinberg and conservative firms. Southworth (forthcoming: 13) reports on a "lawyer who helped establish several religious groups and served at a high level in the Reagan Justice Department [who] worked in a small firm that serves churches and not-for-profit Christian groups and attracts like-minded Christian evangelicals."

While necessary, compatibility is sufficient to sustain small-firm practice only in combination with an adequate financial base and a satisfying agenda. Virtually all small-firm practitioners must subsidize their cause lawyering with income generated by fee-for-service work. Under some circumstances, the fee-for-service caseload can be so heavy as to become the conventional tail wagging the cause lawyering dog. Equally problematic, insofar as fee-for-service clients and cases are on the *wrong* side, the accommodation necessary to maintain the financial viability of the firm will seem self-defeating. Recall the unwillingness of the Marks and Feinberg firm to represent landlords; or imagine the unimaginable: a "born-again" Christian being asked to represent a family-planning clinic.

Another variation on the theme of painful accommodation is provided by an attorney with a civil rights practice—surviving, but just barely, on fees made available by a federal statute for *successful* civil rights litigation. "Part of the headache when I was doing 100 percent civil rights works is the headache of [just trying to make a living]. When you can't make a living, everything else is tainted; everything else is double hard. . . . My C.P.A. said, "[Name], if you want to help those people you've got to change your practice. Sooner or later not only economically you're going down but emotionally you're burning out" (Scheingold and Bloom, 1998: 242–43). After incorporating more business clients into his practice and shifting from civil rights cause lawyering to providing pro bono services for clients who could not afford legal representation, he felt that "tons of weight" had been lifted off of him. However in shifting from civil rights to unmet legal needs, this lawyer arguably recrossed the boundary from cause lawyering to conventional lawyering—at least according to criteria we articulated in Chapter 1.

There are, however, also a variety of situations in which accommodation does not put the rewards of cause lawyering at risk. Personal injury practice seems to provide liberal-left cause lawyers with the most attractive range of options because large settlements can generate working capital and because in the current political climate tort litigation can be politically gratifying. As one attorney put it, these cases can "either change corporate conduct or governmental conduct for the better—in a way that deters others and sometimes punishes wrongdoers of perpetuating a particular practice that is socially reprehensible" (Scheingold and Bloom, 1998: 243). More broadly still, this same attorney sees himself arrayed in battle against the right-wing tort-reform movement. And even when cases have no ascertainable political or social import, being a plaintiff's lawyer in personal injury litigation means being consistently on the right side—or at least not on the wrong side.

So-called critical lawyers (Trubek and Kransberger, 1998) have undertaken a different sort of accommodation—less reprioritizing than reinterpreting the calculus of risk and reward. As it became increasingly difficult for small-firm cause lawyers with left-activist aspirations to locate and contribute to political or social movements of their liking, some have embraced a poststructuralist ideology and shifted the focus of their work to the broad goal of client empowerment. As one lawyer described it, critical lawyering "was a lot more representing people dealing with problems with the system as it is rather than people leading struggles to change it, I guess. You know it goes on but it's more low key and more long term and more individual and less explicitly revolutionary, I guess" (Scheingold and Bloom, 1998: 243).

Arguably, it might be said, making a virtue of necessity, some small-firm cause lawyers thus have taken advantage of the rightward shift in the national political climate to rethink what was important to them. The result is the emergence of critical and largely feminist small-firm practices—with the mission of empowering individual clients and taking comfort from having a direct and immediate impact on their lives (Trubek and Kransberger, 1998).

Conclusion

This chapter has focused on the sites at which cause lawyering is practiced and on the opportunities and constraints found in those sites. Cause lawyering is more than an ideology, a story that lawyers can tell themselves about how their work comports with their beliefs. It is a way of doing things that takes money, time, and strategic ingenuity as well as moral and political commitment. Practice sites help shape and give meaning to cause lawyering and to cause lawyers by making available different opportunities and imposing different costs. They make certain strategic decisions possible, while foreclosing others. They provide the arenas in which lawyers are challenged to animate their work with their political and moral commitments.

Pro bono programs in *corporate firms* offer the most limited rewards for cause lawyers while entailing the fewest career risks. In return for a more than comfortable income, the time open for cause lawyering is very confined, as is the choice of causes and the means to pursue them. In terms of risk and reward, *salaried practice* constitutes the moderate middle in that full-time cause lawyering and a stable and adequate income are assured, but the agenda—that is, the means and ends of cause lawyering—is determined by the priorities of the organization providing the salary. In contrast to the other two practice sites, *small-firm* cause lawyering is a high-stakes game: maximum freedom to choose causes, colleagues, tactics, and strategy, but in a setting that tends to be volatile and insecure.

It is also important to recognize that despite these variable patterns, it is precisely this risk-and-reward structure, this trade-off in possibilities and problems, which distinguishes the career options of cause lawyers from those of conventional lawyers. It is primarily for this reason that we reject the claim that conservative lawyers in corporate practice are, in effect, right-wing *cause* lawyers. While the consonance between their values and their practice is undeniable, corporate lawyering is about embracing the benefits of doing *well* and avoiding the risks endemic to doing *good*. In contrast, cause lawyers must, if they are to do good, be prepared to forgo a measure of material success and professional prestige. Southworth (forthcoming) finds that this is just as true of the right-wing cause lawyers practicing outside corporate firms as it is of the liberal-left adversaries—but is entirely absent from corporate practice as such.

In any case, for each cause lawyer the search for a practice setting that reconciles political beliefs and the demands of legal work is a personal quest. In some cases, the objective is pragmatic and particular, an alternative to the stifling prospect of life as a hired gun. Any worthwhile cause becomes, in effect, a port in the storm—chosen without much reflection and with no ideological or programmatic strings attached. In other instances, cause lawyering reflects serious dedication to a particular objective or to some broader ideal (Sarat, 1998a). Thus, abortion rights may be pursued as ends in themselves or as one element of a feminist political agenda. Similarly, support for tort reform may be based on objections to excessive jury awards or may be a sign of commitment to the property rights movement. The defining attribute of cause lawyering is not how beliefs are reconciled with the demands of practice but rather the simple imperative that they must be reconciled.

In the next chapter, on democratic advocacy, we leave behind these personal, practice-specific accommodations. Individual calculations of risk and reward driving cause lawyers in different settings will take a backseat to the collective import of cause lawyering as a political institution—to cause lawyering's contribution to the creation, defense, and extension of democratic institutions.

Cause Lawyers and Liberal Democracy: On the Possibilities of Democratic Advocacy

CAUSE LAWYERS in the United States, as we have demonstrated, work within three *professional* contexts—the organized bar, law schools, and legal practice. In this chapter we go on to consider the larger *political* context of cause lawyering—a context shaped by the values of liberal democracy. The institutional practices that democracy makes available to cause lawyers both constrain and enable their efforts to translate controversial ethical commitments into political achievements. Cause lawyering, then, may rightly be labeled as one kind of democratic advocacy.

Lawyers have long been thought to play important roles in democratic politics, serving in disproportionate numbers as public officials and contributing to a political culture conducive to the maintenance and reproduction of democratic virtues. Alexis de Tocqueville's (1876: 348) classic analysis of the ways lawyers and the legal profession helped mitigate the tyranny of the majority was, and remains, a touchstone for thinking about democratic advocacy. He pointed to "habits of order, a taste for formalities, and a kind of instinctive regard for the regular connection of ideas" which would help make lawyers a calming counterweight to "the unreflecting passions of the multitude" (1876: 349). Tocqueville also saw in the legal profession an "aristocratic" element necessary to the health and well-being of democratic society. As he put it, "Without this admixture of lawyer-like sobriety with the democratic principle, I question whether democratic institutions could long be maintained" (1876: 352).

More recently, important research has pointed to the roles lawyers play in constructing and maintaining the institutions that make democracy work (see Halliday and Karpik, 1997). As Terence Halliday (1998a: 259) recently noted, "A mounting body of scholarship demonstrates that the fortunes of legal professions and states are intertwined. It stimulates investigation of the hypothesis that there is a reciprocity of relationships between those occupations which claim a monopoly of expertise and the states which must rely on that expertise to govern." This scholarship calls on us to examine links between professions and politics at the level of practices and activities—to consider the kinds of advocacy lawyers undertake and the things they advocate. It asks us to look at what lawyers do in the political, not just in the professional, arena.

From Halliday's (1998a: 261) perspective, lawyers have played, and continue to play, key roles in advancing three aspects of what he calls "political liberalism," namely "the construction of a moderate state; the creation of citizenship rights; and the development of civil society." Lawyers are important advocates for constitutional government and separation of state powers, and they contribute variously to the "expansion and defense of citizenship rights" (Halliday, 1998a: 270). In this and in their work in voluntary associations, the representation of publics, and their cultivation of "civic virtue," lawyers develop a civil society of the kind Tocqueville (1876) thought essential to democracy (Halliday 1998a: 266–67).

This chapter follows Tocqueville's (1876) and Halliday's (1998a) lead in looking at what cause lawyers do *to* and *for* liberal democracy and what liberal democracy means for the cause lawyering enterprise. For Tocqueville, the question would be whether cause lawyers are more like their traditional lawyer colleagues in their "habits of mind" or whether their commitment to making a profession of their beliefs undoes their stabilizing contribution to liberal democracy. As for Halliday (1998a: 272), he is right to differentiate what he calls "liberal advocacy lawyering" from "radical cause lawyering" as a first step in understanding the possibilities and pitfalls of democratic advocacy in liberal societies. However, the relations of cause lawyering and liberal democracy are somewhat more complex than that distinction can capture. Cause lawyers pursue a puzzling mix of competing and convergent democratic aspirations that need careful examination.

The resultant complexities emerge once we acknowledge the difference between left-wing and right-wing cause lawyers, on the one hand, and between those who support or oppose liberal democracy, on the other hand. While the left-right divide is readily comprehensible and seems at first glance the more politically salient, the division between cause lawyers who work for liberal democracy and those who challenge it tells us more about the dilemmas of democratic advocacy in the United States. If we are to understand the phenomenon of democratic advocacy, we must examine the ways in which some cause lawyers link the causes they represent to the health of liberal democracy while others act in opposition to it.

In addition, and especially telling for this chapter, we will explore the way democracy both energizes and constrains the aspirations of cause lawyers. Not surprisingly, successful cause lawyering comes more easily to those who work on behalf of liberal democracy—irrespective of whether they lean to the left or to the right. By the same token, lawyers who challenge liberal democracy—those with radical and transformative commitments—tend to find themselves facing difficult choices. Throughout this chapter, we will look carefully at precisely how, why, and to what extent this is the case.

A Note on Left- and Right-Wing Cause Lawyering

Until recently, when right-wing cause lawyering emerged from the political and academic shadows, cause lawyering was generally understood as a vehicle of the left (Bachmann, 1984–85). Indeed, its origins in the United States can be reasonably traced to the National Association of Colored People (NAACP) (St. James, 1958) and the American Civil Liberties Union (ACLU) (Walker, 1992)—both of which began to function in the early twentieth century. Their left-of-center focus was characteristic of virtually all cause lawyering until roughly the 1980s. At that time cause lawyering on the right made its appearance and since then has become increasingly prominent and influential (see Carter, 2001; and Teles, 2003).

Despite the caveats expressed above, the left-right divide provides a useful starting point for shifting from the professional terrain of Chapter 4 to the political terrain of Chapter 5. Pursuing the distinction between left-wing and right-wing lawyering makes it immediately clear that *cause lawyering is a political project*. This distinction is useful in identifying the affiliations and affinities that are likely to develop among cause lawyers, political parties, interest groups, and social movements. Finally, thinking in terms of left and right suggests that the fortunes of cause lawyers are likely to ebb and flow along with changes in the political climate—and thus with the fortunes of their allies and adversaries.

Useful as it is, however, the distinction between the left and the right is too crude to adequately capture the multiple democratic visions driving cause lawyers in this country. Similarly, to think solely in terms of left and right obscures the most important determinants of successful advocacy by cause lawyers within liberal democracy. If we are to understand those visions and the relative success that lawyers attain in realizing them, it is necessary to explore, alongside the division between left and right, cleavages within liberal democratic advocacy and between liberal democracy and its opponents.

Liberal Democracy and Its Transformative Adversaries

While their *democratic aspirations* are manifest and pervasive, cause lawyers pursue dramatically different democratic dreams. There are at least six thematic variations in cause lawyering's democratic agenda. Cause lawyers committed to liberal democracy divide along what we will call left-liberal, neoliberal, and libertarian lines. Those who challenge liberal democracy fall into social-democratic, emancipatory-democratic, and evangelical-democratic camps. While some of these terms are more familiar than others, we will briefly summarize each of them in order to indicate how they relate to democratic values and to one another.

In its classic sense, as well as in today's common usage, liberal democracy is identified with representative government, the rule of law, individual rights (including private property), and an autonomous, open, and pluralistic civil society (Levine, 1981; Pennock and Chapman, 1983). According to David Held (1995), individual rights are crucial to the transformation of a constitutional (or rule-of-law) state into a liberal democracy. Whereas a constitutional state "circumscribes power and provides a regulatory mechanism and checks on rulers and ruled alike, in a democratic state 'rulers' are representatives of, and accountable to, citizens" (Held, 1995: 149). One element necessary for establishing accountability is the introduction of individual rights as a way of constituting citizens and citizenship within a political community (Thompson, 1990).

The specifically liberal democratic rights which Held (1995) had in mind are often identified as "first-generation" rights. They tend to be negative—directed at limiting interference by the state and other social actors and protecting liberty, private property, privacy, due process, and the like (see Berlin, 1958). However, first-generation rights also include rights to political participation—freedom to speak, run for office, vote, and so on. In the aggregate, first-generation rights are both the hallmark and the bulwark of the classic liberal democratic vision of a politically accountable rule-of-law state which nurtures and serves a robust and autonomous civil society (Halliday, 1998a). In sum, liberal democracy is rooted in a combination of civil and political rights that invest citizens in, and protect them from, the state.

As is readily apparent, first-generation rights are largely indistinguishable from the rights guaranteed by the United States Constitution. This point is important because they are the means, as well as the ends, of liberal democratic cause lawyering. Rights litigation is the primary agent of liberal democratic cause lawyering, and the preservation and extension of these rights is their mission (Scheingold, 1974; McCann, 1994). Accordingly, insofar as the means and ends of liberal democracy are institutionalized in constitutional, political, and legal process, liberal democratic cause lawyers are in a privileged position—in sharp contrast to the marginalized circumstances of their more radical counterparts.

Opposition to liberal democracy among cause lawyers in the United States comes from two different directions: social and emancipatory democrats *on the left*, as well as evangelical Christians *on the right*. They each have objections to first-generation rights and offer programs which supplement, transcend, or *repudiate* these rights. In this sense, evangelical Christians as well as social and emancipatory democrats pursue *transformative* agendas—albeit to different degrees and for different reasons (see, e.g., Cronin, 1992).

Social democracy does not involve a repudiation of the procedural imperatives of first-generation rights, even though it deems them insufficient as a means for achieving a just society and as its defining ends. Instead, social democracy is directed at supplementing first-generation procedural rights with the material imperatives of second-generation rights to economic and social well-being—including, for example, education, health care, minimum income, secure employment, workplace organization, food, housing, social security (Hicks, 1999). As Held (1995: 69) explains, social democracy entails "redistributive welfare measures—including measures introducing social security, public health provision and new forms of progressive taxation."

Social democracy thus emerges as a *"third way"* between liberal democracy and socialism. Whereas the former aspires primarily to free individuals and civil society from an abusive and nonaccountable state, the core aspiration of social democracy is to redress material privation (Hicks, 1999). Whereas socialism aspires to provide this same redress through the abolition of private property and ultimately the state itself, social democracy seeks to deploy an accountable and inclusive state to promote material equality. In short, social democracy aspires to transform liberal democracy's procedural pluralism, with its promise of equal opportunity, into an outcome-oriented pluralism which enhances substantive equality as well as providing procedural protections.

The central problematic for social democratic cause lawyering in the twenty-first century is that second-generation rights have been selectively, grudgingly, and only episodically accepted (Rabinowitz, 1996; Reisman, 1999). They were introduced into mainstream political discourse in the United States by the Progressive movement in the early twentieth century and subsequently extended and institutionalized by the New Deal in the 1930s and by the Great Society programs of the 1960s and 1970s. More recently they have been under sharp attack (Thody, 1995).

But both political and legal battles on behalf of second-generation rights have always been very much an uphill struggle. Nor is there any constitutional mandate that protects second-generation rights and which can be made into the subject of constitutional litigation. Legislation that was enacted as part of one political program can be taken away under another, leaving cause lawyers with social democratic aspirations the difficult choice between fighting for procedural—that is, liberal democratic—remedies or undertaking political mobilization against the prevailing political tide (see, e.g., Norris and Thompson, 1995).

Emancipatory democracy is a concept developed recently by Boaventura de Sousa Santos (1995), but it is rooted in the radical egalitarian tradition of Rousseau, Marx, and others. Put another way, emancipatory democracy serves as the postmodern voice of utopian aspirations.[1] Indeed, Santos himself sees emancipatory democracy in terms of a "radically democratic, socialist society" (1995: 240)—radical in that it repudiates all forms of power, no matter how well intended its objectives, and democratic in its goal of an egalitarian, participatory, and decentralized political society (see Barber, 1984).[2] The locus of emancipatory political democracy is, therefore, shifted to small-scale and participatory institutions. Whereas the Marxian left aspired to create a mass movement driven by a particular ideology and dedicated to achieving its substantive objectives, emancipatory democracy eschews both power and overarching narratives—be they liberal democratic or Marxist. It follows that emancipatory democracy also eschews first- and second-generation rights since each relies on the state for their realization—albeit in different ways and to different degrees.[3] In their place, Santos constructs visions of democracy and law that celebrate dispersion, subversion, indeterminacy, and codependence, while being deeply distrustful of order, regularity, coherence, and coordination.

The postmodern vision of legality that emerges substitutes mediation for regulation and nurtures reciprocity and mutuality (Unger, 1976). The implications for cause lawyering are profound—although not addressed by Santos. To forswear the institutional apparatus that links rights claims to remedies is to put impact litigation, the preferred instrument of liberal democratic cause lawyering and indeed liberal rights themselves, at bay. Similarly, but more profoundly, to sanctify concepts of justice and democracy as open-ended and forever out of reach is, in effect, to repudiate ideals traditionally associated with law, lawyers, and the legal profession.

Still, we detect emancipatory themes among a so-called critical cohort of cause lawyers. Their work will be discussed below. Suffice it to say at this point that in the spirit of emancipatory democracy, critical cause lawyering is focused on the microsites of power and on intervention in the daily lives of marginalized Americans. There is, we will argue, reason to be skeptical about the transformative potential of critical cause lawyering in part because it rejects efforts to construct comprehensive, coherent, and coordinated social movements.

Evangelical democracy repudiates not only first-generation rights but rights per se as a cornerstone of politics and society (Soper, 1994). The problem with rights is that they are secular and individualistic, and they privilege personal entitlement. In contrast, evangelicals emphasize personal responsibility to a community united by a commitment to biblical injunctions. "As defined by the leaders of the Religious Right, morality is the moral code of Christian fundamentalism.

Christian fundamentalists believe that the Bible is to be read literally, not symbolically, with every word taken to express the will of God. This is why they protest against the teaching of evolutionary theory in the public schools, for instance, and why they generally decry the growth of secular humanism" (Ball and Dagger, 1995: 117).

The evangelical political movement challenges fundamental tenets of liberal democracy: neutrality as to ultimate ends and a dispassionate and inclusive pluralism wedded to the separation between church and state. Accordingly, targets of evangelical political mobilization include the family, education, the media, the courts, and of course, the political arena itself—with the goal of imbuing all of these basic institutions with biblical values (Trembath, 1987). The evangelical challenge is thus transformative: "What is ultimately at issue are deeply rooted and fundamentally different understandings of being and purpose" (Hunter, 1991: 128). In sum, the evangelical movement does not just oppose liberal democracy but is at war with it—a so-called *culture war*.

However, all this begs a crucial question. In what sense is it *democratic* to construct a political society steeped in biblical morality and resting on biblical authority? To its evangelical proponents, democracy means being accountable to a *moral*, not a numerical, majority. "The Religious Right . . . claims to be democratic, by which it means that society should follow the lead of a righteous or 'moral' majority of Christians" (Ball and Dagger, 1995: 117).

In naming his incipient movement the Moral Majority, Jerry Falwell was in effect charting both its objectives and its modus operandi. Since then the evangelical right has been intensively engaged in politics of all kinds: elections, lobbying, political action committees, and grassroots organizing through churches (Liebman and Wuthnow, 1983). Of course, the success of this mobilization is determined not by whether it encompasses a majority of the entire electorate, but by how influential it becomes in altering political discourse, electoral results, and policy decisions so as to reflect evangelical Protestant values. Similarly, the goal of the cause lawyers who manage "evangelical legal mobilization" (Den Dulk, n.d.: 1) is to infuse constitutional discourse and decisions with those same values.

So far we have presented an overview of the several variants of cause lawyering's democratic agenda in order to set the context for the extended analysis which follows. Below we classify cause lawyering practices according to our scheme of democracy advocacy. To do so is, however, more difficult than it might seem to be. For example, First Amendment cause lawyering appears at first glance to be *liberal democratic*. However, evangelical cause lawyers may mobilize the First Amendment in pursuit of their *transformative* agenda. Similarly, while some cause lawyers pursue the transformative goal of abolishing capital punishment, others simply seek the liberal democratic goal of ensuring fair trials in death penalty cases. In sorting out cause lawyers according to their targets and tactics, it is, therefore, necessary to consider not only their *goals* but also their *motives*.

Further complicating our analysis is the relationship between targets and tactics. Not only is liberal democratic cause lawyering privileged and, thus, the line of least resistance, but it constitutes, in addition, a kind of magnetic field which attracts even those cause lawyers who wish to challenge liberalism (Cain, 2000). Opponents of liberal democracy are drawn into that field for strategic reasons—deploying liberal means and even seeking liberal ends for their immediate, if ultimately unsatisfactory, benefits.

Lawyering for Liberal Democracy

As we have already suggested, traditional cause lawyering is associated with a legal and political vision of liberal democracy—and, thus, with first-generation rights (Casper, 1972). What liberals share is a distrust of the state and a faith in first-generation rights as necessary and sufficient protection against its unwarranted intrusions into civil society. What divides liberals is the choice of which first-generation rights they privilege and which they tend to disregard.

There are three cohorts of liberal cause lawyers. Neoliberals focus almost exclusively on property rights (MacEwan, 1999). Libertarians cast their net somewhat more widely by advocating the full range of what we will call *private* first-generation rights, which taken together constitute the liberal democratic concept of individual freedom (Machan, 1974). Libertarians tend to ignore *political* rights, which protect consent and accountability in the American democracy. Left-liberals reverse these priorities and are, not surprisingly, likely to put their energy into rights which are associated with protecting the integrity of the political order. For neoliberal and libertarian cause lawyers, civil society is an end in itself, whereas for left-liberals civil society is a means to an end—*an* aspiration but not *the* aspiration of liberal democracy.

Neoliberal and Libertarian Lawyering

We include in our neoliberal category cause lawyers whose primary mission is to defend and extend property rights in order to transfer "power from government regulators to landowners and entrepreneurs" (Heinz, Paik, and Southworth, 2003: 8). Their advocacy is conducted in conjunction with a variety of organizations, all of which are funded by corporate interests: the Pacific Legal Foundation, the Manhattan Institute, and the Mountain States Legal Foundation, to mention only three of most well known.[4] Their chosen targets include tort reform, environment regulation, land use regulation, and so forth. In each of these areas they believe that they are not simply defending material interests but the American liberal democratic tradition itself. They see themselves, in Laura Hatcher's words (forthcoming: 2), as protecting "the heart of the liberalism that informs the U.S. constitutional system: the use of property as a means of checking state power."

Libertarians, unlike neoliberals, look beyond property rights and the protection of business interests to individual liberties in the social and cultural spheres. Thus, Ann Southworth (forthcoming: 17) tells of a lawyer who had been tortured as a prisoner of war in Vietnam and who saw the right to self-defense (and thus the right to own guns) as "a natural right of a human being by virtue of his birth." Similarly, libertarians, but not neoliberals, tend to oppose criminalization where there is no identifiable victim—such as using drugs and viewing pornography (Boaz, 1997). In short, libertarians emphasize a wide range of individual freedoms and, as a result, sometimes find common cause with left-leaning civil liberties lawyers.

Still, the boundary which separates libertarian from neoliberal cause lawyering is both porous and disputed. Hatcher's (forthcoming: 5) characterization of neoliberals as "economic libertarians" identifies both common ground and divergence in these categories. Similarly, Southworth (forthcoming: 18–19) reports that

> several libertarians identified their constituency as disadvantaged minorities thwarted in their entrepreneurial ambitions by burdensome regulation. Another libertarian lawyer described himself as a champion of consumers harmed by misguided regulation—e.g., the FDA's slow approval process for new drugs that might save lives, and the National Highway Transportation Safety Administration's fuel emissions standards, which encourage Detroit to produce smaller (and less safe) automobiles.[5]

Hatcher (forthcoming: 22) observed an analogous convergence in the Institute for Justice, which, in her words, "claims to be the only true libertarian law group, and proclaims itself as the best defender of civil rights and liberties throughout the political spectrum." While its primary mission has been to build the "takings clause" of the Fifth Amendment into a bulwark of property rights, the Institute for Justice is also identified with the broader libertarian agenda—working on behalf of school choice, welfare reform, and interracial adoption while opposing mandatory community service (Hatcher, forthcoming: 22). In short, libertarians are often concerned about property rights and neoliberals are likely to be sympathetic to efforts to reduce government intervention in the society as well as in the economy. Finally, both libertarians and neoliberals are guided in the choices they make by the ideology of equal opportunity, which they see as the essential organizing principle for civil society.

Lawyering for the Liberal Left

While neoliberals privilege protection of property rights and libertarians embrace a much wider range of the private rights of individuals, left-liberals defend the *public*, as well as the private, rights of individuals. In other words, the left-liberal agenda is not only more comprehensive than that of libertarians and neoliberals. More tellingly, left-liberal cause lawyers advocate for rights which support a robust and inclusive form of political and social citizenship (Kramer, 1972).

One prototypical voice of left-liberal cause lawyering illustrates the commitment to what we are calling public rights. The American Civil Liberties Union (ACLU) is fond of claiming the entire Bill of Rights as its client.[6] This claim is an exaggeration only in the sense that property rights are largely excluded from its agenda. Otherwise, the ACLU is concerned with protecting civil society from unwarranted intrusions and thus is inclined, like libertarians, to oppose laws which restrict religious freedom, sexual practices, drug use, gambling, and the like. But the ACLU is also an especially determined defender of those provisions of the Constitution that protect electoral accountability—most notably First Amendment rights to free speech and assembly (see Casper, 1972; and Downs, 1985).

There are, of course, multiple targets of left-liberal cause lawyering. Among these targets are immigration practices, the death penalty, police violence, the right to die, the rights of prisoners, employment discrimination, tenant rights, restrictions on abortion, and so on (Kelly, 1994: 145–63). It is clear why all of these are targets of the liberal-left rather than neoliberal or libertarian cause lawyers. Further probing is necessary, however, to locate the boundary between the liberal-left and the transformative-left—associated with social democracy and emancipatory democracy, both of which we consider below.

This boundary has less to do with the targets per se than with underlying objectives—a point that is illustrated in work on behalf of the homeless by Washington State's Evergreen Legal Services Program. One of the program's attorneys found it especially gratifying to serve "homeless alcoholic psychotic street people who are regularly screwed over" in the legal, legislative, and corporate systems. Yet he fully realizes the limitations of this kind of work. "I [am] pragmatic in the sense that I try to achieve little victories where I can for clients. But ultimately that makes me a conservative because I'm not trying to overthrow the system. So I'm liberal in the sense that I'm trying to get victories where I can within the framework of the system, but I'm not doing something radical outside the system" (Scheingold and Bloom, 1998: 230).[7] We agree with this lawyer's self-description as pragmatic and liberal because he targets the symptoms of dispossession rather than mounting a more ambitious campaign to alter the political direction of the United States—although in our scheme he would, of course, be classified as *left*-liberal.

In sum, left-liberal cause lawyering is defined by its commitment to building an inclusive civil society, to protecting democratic institutions, and to providing fair treatment for those subject to the state's awesome power to deprive them of liberty and even life (see Cain, 2000; and López, 1992). Most of the requisite rights are explicitly written into the Constitution—whether as rights per se or as provisions which define the institutional responsibilities of the three branches of the government and the division of power and responsibility between states and the federal government. Accordingly liberal democratic cause lawyering has ready access to constitutional discourse and to leverage afforded by litigation (Casper, 1972; Greenberg, 1994; Epp, 1998). For all these reasons, it makes good sense to think of the left-liberal cause lawyering agenda as intrinsic to, and sustained by, liberal democracy in the United States.

Patterns of inclusion and exclusion within the rights agendas of the liberal cause lawyers whom we have considered so far certainly do *not* reflect a division of labor among allies collectively committed to first-generation rights. Instead, these patterns reveal competing visions of the American democracy. For both libertarians and neoliberals pursuing a "let the chips fall where they may" version of equal opportunity, civil society is the source of virtue and enterprise while the government is a threat to both. In contrast to this intense focus on the private sphere, left-liberals pursue a more political and public vision of liberal democracy. For them, first-generation rights are not ends in themselves but means to be used in guarding the integrity of the political process and ensuring the inclusiveness of civil society. In short, left-liberalism is about constructing a particular kind of polis (Feinberg, 1998). For libertarian and neoliberal cause lawyers, individual freedom and an autonomous civil society are *both necessary and sufficient* conditions of a healthy democratic order.

For all of the distinctions among them, however, there is strategic common ground which tends to put liberal cause lawyers on equal footing while providing them with an advantage over cause lawyers who challenge liberal democracy. As we have already suggested, liberal cause lawyers work from within well-entrenched constitutional discourse. They also contribute to the legitimacy of both the legal profession and American democracy. Accordingly, for a combination of expressive and instrumental reasons, litigation is very much the hallmark of liberal democratic cause lawyering. Litigation works for them—not because they always can count on winning, but because they can count on being accepted as players—whether in judicial proceedings or while bargaining in "the shadow of the law" (Mnookin and Kornhauser, 1979). In addition, as liberals they believe in the moral sufficiency and political efficacy of the rights in which their litigation is rooted.

Cause lawyers who challenge liberalism, whom we will discuss in the next section, have a much more ambivalent relationship to rights—in particular to first-generation rights. They are rights skeptics—or in some instances rights cynics (see, e.g., Morgan, 1984). Rather than embracing the "myth of rights" (Scheingold, 1974) as do the liberals, they distrust rights. This distrust stems not only from the practical difficulty of incorporating rights strategies into their challenges to liberal democracy but also from the belief that achieving rights would betray their purposes rather than further them. Nonetheless, as we have already suggested, they are often drawn to rights strategies as last resorts, by desperation rather than by expectation.

Lawyering Against Liberal Democracy

While cause lawyering and liberal democracy are, in many respects, inextricably enmeshed with one another, some cause lawyers challenge liberal democracy's core premises and projects. On the left, the aspirations are egalitarian—directed at substituting equality of outcomes for liberal democracy's embrace of equal opportunity. Cause lawyers on the left have pursued two distinctly different paths toward equalization: a social-democratic path, which privileges the state, and an emancipatory-democratic vision, which views the state as inescapably problematic. On the right, the goal is to move away from liberal democracy's commitment to individualism and personal freedom—substituting for it a vision of personal responsibility in the service of moral community. While moral community can be constructed from secular sources, in the United States today right-wing cause lawyers challenge liberalism in biblical terms from within the evangelical-Protestant movement.

In spelling this out in more detail, our first goal is to indicate how, why, and to what extent lawyers representing the transformative-left and the transformative-right challenge the liberal democratic paradigm. In addition to specifying how each of these variants of cause lawyering differs from one another and from their liberal democratic counterparts, we also want to demonstrate that each of these opponents of liberal democracy faces similar strategic trade-offs. On the one hand, they can pursue robust versions of their respective ideologies at the cost of marginalizing themselves. Alternatively, they can "liberalize" and narrow their approach in order to take advantage of the leverage available to liberal democratic cause lawyering.

Evangelical Advocacy

It might seem that all Christian cause lawyering would be equally outside liberal democracy's commitment to a secular state and an inclusive civil society. It is important, however, to distinguish the legal arm of the evangelical political movement from cause lawyering which is simply inspired by Christian religious values. Whereas the former directly challenges liberal democracy, the latter need not be uncomfortable with either liberalism's means or its ends.

Southworth (forthcoming: 14) calls attention to religiously motivated attorneys who behave like liberal democratic cause lawyers and see themselves as working within "the liberal activist tradition." Like all cause lawyers they seek consonance between their personal values and their legal practice—all the while marching to a different drummer. Consider this account of the decision to become a lawyer: "A lot of prayer went into it. As a Christian person it was important to me . . . that I do things that seem to be in the service of God." In addition, they are driven by specifiable objections to discrete social harms. In this vein, Southworth (forthcoming: 21–22) describes an attorney who defended parental notification requirements for abortion from his perspective as a parent—reasoning that he would want to be notified if his daughter sought an abortion. Another of Southworth's (forthcoming: 22) respondents explained that he came to view pornography as socially harmful on the basis of evidence he encountered while working in a prosecutor's office. In this version of Christian cause lawyering, religious values are a matter of *personal conscience*, which in turn influences calculations of social harm.

"Evangelical Protestant legal mobilization" (Den Dulk, n.d.: 1) is another thing entirely. To begin with, attorneys who serve the evangelical movement tend to see their lawyering as a thoroughly religious calling (Brown, 2002). Southworth (forthcoming: 16) provides numerous examples of such lawyers, including a lawyer who was drawn into opposition to abortion after being "called by the highest power to do justice and serve our fellow men and women." Similarly, Kevin den Dulk (n.d.: 13) discusses a church-state attorney who "believed he heard a divine voice say, 'I am your client,' which led him to rethink his vocational plans." Evangelical Christians come to cause lawyering as one aspect of being "born again"—through "epiphanies" drawing them into "service to God." Their cause lawyering is a product of religious revelation and an instrument of personal redemption. "For evangelical attorneys the meanings of a cause are embedded in a religious worldview; causes are defined relative to beliefs about the nature and limits of state power, the authority and integrity of the institutional church, and about the primacy of individual salvation" (Den Dulk, n.d.: 2).[8]

Even more important for our purposes, Den Dulk (n.d.) documents how evangelical legal mobilization is linked to a coherent and influential political movement with a clearly theocratic agenda (Noll, 2001). He traces this *legal* mobilization directly to the evangelical *political* mobilization undertaken by Jerry Falwell's Moral Majority in the 1970s. The starting point for it was "a religious understanding of society's moral failures: alcohol or dancing, creeping socialism, or, more recently, abortion, pornography, declining schools, and same-sex marriage" (Den Dulk, n.d.: 8). Den Dulk (n.d.: 8) notes that "many evangelicals envisioned the world as divided in two: the majority of citizens, who were devoted to the Judeo-Christian values of the past, and the powerful secular minority trying to foist its will on the rest of society. Evangelical leaders hoped that they could mobilize the silent majority to redeem culture by freeing it from the pernicious influence of the godless elite."

Legal mobilization was, in effect, a product of, and a partner in, political mobilization and led to the creation of a large number of organizations dedicated to evangelical Protestant cause lawyering (Brown, 2002). Among these organizations were the Christian Legal Society, the Rutherford Institute, Christian Advocates Serving Evangelism, the Home School Legal Defense Association, and the Center for Law and Religious Freedom.

Den Dulk (n.d.:15–25) usefully calls attention to a division of labor among these organizations, with some pursuing a "defensive" strategy dedicated to protecting cultural space while others undertake an offensive strategy devoted to overcoming the corruption of contemporary culture. The defensive strategy trades limited objectives for ready access to first-generation rights discourse. The offensive strategy, in sharp contrast, is not limited to defending cultural space from the state but instead aims "to carve out a cultural space that provides fewer obstacles to moral and spiritual purity" (Den Dulk, n.d.: 15).

The defensive strategy is tethered to, but not derived from, the First Amendment's protection of religious freedom (Brown, 2002). Secular principles of religious freedom are invoked not as ends in themselves but to serve the theocratic purposes of the Moral Majority. Thus, Den Dulk (n.d.: 15) reports that the Christian Law Association (CLA) was created by the Moral Majority in 1977 "to resist nearly all governmental regulation of fundamentalist schools and churches. CLA attorneys argued that governmental authority in the life of the church was severely circumscribed by the Constitution." This ostensibly secular objective was, however, "rooted in a religious understanding of parental obligations: God requires parents to educate according to religious principles, not curricular requirements imposed by the state" (Den Dulk, n.d.: 16).

So, it might reasonably be argued that the defensive strategy deploys liberal rights on behalf of theocratic aspirations and in opposition to liberal democratic values. Still, because the means are liberal democratic, the defensive aspirations of evangelical legal mobilization are, in the final analysis, both facilitated and compromised by its engagement with the liberal democratic constitutional process (Epstein, 1985).

The offensive strategy of the evangelical Protestant movement directly challenges liberal democracy—using a theocratic template to fashion a campaign against "rampant problems" in society: drugs, violence, teenage pregnancy, sexually transmitted disease, and so on (Den Dulk, n.d.:17). The offensive strategy has included efforts by Pat Robertson's American Center for Law and Justice (ACLJ) to return prayer to the public schools and the opposition of the ACLJ as well as other groups to "abortion, assisted suicide, and other 'life issues'" (Den Dulk, n.d.: 23).

This agenda diverges from liberal democratic cause lawyering both with respect to the ends sought and the means deployed. Here the objective is to bring the Judeo-Christian tradition into the state (Noll, 2001). If evangelical cause lawyers had their way, enforcement of religious values would become a central responsibility of the state (Brown, 2002). "Liberal theory and practice have often assumed that religionists may enjoy their freedom as long as they keep religious practice a private affair. Many evangelicals, however, cannot abide by such an arrangement. They seek more than cultural space to practice religion in private; they wish to transform the culture as a whole by using public means to influence individual behavior and direct others toward their understanding of God's will" (Den Dulk, n.d.: 22). Cause lawyers serving the evangelical movement are, in effect, dedicated to establishing (to put the best possible face on it) an *ecumenical theocracy*.

Given these ends, it is not surprising that the legal as opposed to political means available to them are somewhat circumscribed. Opposition to abortion and support for prayer in the public schools puts evangelical attorneys at odds with prevailing constitutional law (Epstein, 1985), though it may win them considerable support within the Republican Party. The result is, at least tactically speaking, to relegate evangelical cause lawyers to the constitutional sidelines. While they are no longer, according to Den Dulk (n.d.: 24–25), engaged in abortion and school prayer litigation, they have become "defenders of the defenders." Somewhat paradoxically, then, while the current political climate opens up avenues for successful advocacy within legislative and administrative arenas, the offensive strategy of the evangelical legal mobilization tends to put its cause lawyers on the defensive—literally and figuratively.

Lawyering for the Transformative-Left

The National Lawyers Guild (NLG), through its resolute pursuit of alternatives to liberal democratic visions of the state, corporate enterprise, and the legal profession, has been the bulwark of transformative-left cause lawyering in the United States for a long time.[9] Neither the Guild's mandate nor the agenda of lawyers on the transformative-left has now, or ever has had, the ideological or organizational coherence of the current evangelical legal mobilization

(Scheingold, 1998). However, in the late 1960s and early 1970s there was at least a kind of coherence—or perhaps more accurately an *imagined* coherence. Its symbolic embodiment was *The Movement*— an amorphous construct comprising the civil rights, antiwar, and antipoverty movements (Rabinowitz, 1996). All of these elements were viewed as synergistically contributing to a more just, egalitarian, and democratic society. There was a companion tendency to identify *The Movement* with Marxism or socialism more generally—albeit with an amorphous and decidedly nondoctrinaire vision of socialism. The NLG was the legal center of this imagined movement—providing its members with professional sanctuary and ideological leadership.

While the Guild remains the institutional locus of transformative-left lawyering in the United States, both its context and its practices have been dramatically altered by the rightward shift in American politics at the beginning of the 1980s and the collapse of socialism at the end of that decade. America's right turn enhanced the sense of urgency within the transformative-left while reducing its opportunities. At the same time the collapse of socialism generated ideological malaise. As one cause lawyer said, "One of the reasons I think that you don't see a lot of good political law suits—you know, there's no movements, there's no nothing" (Scheingold, 1998: 136).[10] Put in somewhat different terms, the sense of belonging to something bigger—*The Movement*—that sustained the transformative-left in the early days has been lost.

It is not that there is a shortage of worthwhile causes with transformative potential. There are many such causes being pursued by transformative-left cause lawyers: the death penalty (Sarat, 1998a, 2001), wages and working conditions (McCann, 1994; Bloom, 2001), immigration (Coutin, 2001), landlord-tenant conflict (Kelly, 1994), as well as legal practice itself (Trubek and Kransberger, 1998; Scheingold 1998). There is, however, much less optimism about what can be achieved by way of litigation or in the political arena. In addition, there is virtually no sense that the causes are synergistically and transformationally linked to one another. In sum, the perceptions of unity and of imminent success have been drained from transformative-left cause lawyering. Ideological coherence provided by socialism has, in effect, given way to competing visions and dramatically different cause lawyering practices. We characterize the competing visions as social-democratic and emancipatory-democratic.

Social-democratic cause lawyers practice a "politics writ large" (Halliday and Karpik, 1997: 3). They target the state and corporate power, material inequality in any and all of its manifestations, exclusionary practices, and the like. Because constitutional litigation does not serve their purposes very well, these lawyers have turned in different directions—most notably to political mobilization.[11]

Michael McCann's (1994) research on pay equity demonstrates how and under what conditions cause lawyers can combine constitutional litigation with *political mobilization* to destabilize entrenched liberal democratic practices and understandings. Pay equity recognizes and seeks to correct gender bias in the job market—most notably the undervaluation of what traditionally has been women's work. As such, pay equity goes well beyond the liberal democratic standard of equal pay for equal work. McCann (1994) discovered that although pay equity was not established as the guiding principle of wage compensation, defeats in the judicial arena could be leveraged for movement building. Essential in this regard was a cadre of union activists. "The key actors," McCann (1994: 279) argues, "were not judges but movement organizers, who skillfully utilized litigation in a wide variety of movement building activities." McCann (1994: 281) also argues that "the political advances (of the pay equity movement) in many contexts matched or exceeded wage gains. One important advance was at the level of rights consciousness. . . . Legal rights thus became increasingly meaningful both as a general moral discourse and as a strategic resource for ongoing challenges to the status quo power relations." The principal legacy of the pay equity campaign was political, not legal or material.[12]

Today the *civil justice* system may well be the primary site of social democratic cause lawyering aimed at curbing the power of corporations (Hans, 2000). Cause lawyers now are using personal injury litigation explicitly as part of a political attack on corporate prerogatives. This litigation includes efforts to establish corporate liability for such harmful products as tobacco, asbestos, lead paint, and so forth. Also included are attacks on such corporate misbehavior as violating rules against the dumping of toxic materials, exporting of jobs, and mistreatment of workers employed overseas by American corporations (see Litvin, 2003). The broader implications are readily apparent to cause-oriented personal injury attorneys. As one such Seattle lawyer put it, "I've done toxic tort cases here and some civil rights law, some employment discrimination cases. And toxic torts you can get into generally—this idea of a sort of corporate America exposing people heedlessly to toxic substances and people dying from it and everything. So I can get into it on a political level" (Scheingold, 1998: 133).

Insofar as this litigation is coordinated and politicized, the relevant organization is the Trial Lawyers for Public Justice (TLPJ), which visualizes the civil justice system as an instrument of movement building. According to a prominent TLPJ official in private practice,

Public justice is not limited to trial lawyering. In fact it's predominantly a consumer movement. It's predominantly the environmental movement, the women's movement, the civil rights movement, all the various movements that we brought together. So it's not going to be the TLPJ that to me is the movement. It's going to be the TLPJ as part of a public interest movement of activists and lawyers. That's where I see the shape of things to come in the 1990s and the next century. And we're taking steps to build that alliance. (Scheingold, 1998: 35)[13]

Another variation on the social-democratic theme, as well as the constraining pull of liberal-legalism on cause lawyers, is revealed in Austin Sarat's (1998a) research on cause lawyering to abolish the death penalty. Abolitionists view the death penalty as an evil in its own right. But some also see their challenges to it as part of a broadscale effort to curtail other forms of law's violence with their disproportionate and exclusionary impact on marginalized segments of society. However, having reached the unwelcome conclusion that abolition was, in the near future, a *lost* cause (Sarat, 1998b), death penalty opponents shifted their focus.

Rather than looking to outright abolition of the death penalty and using it as a first step in a comprehensive effort to limit or end other forms of law's violence, death penalty lawyers shifted to less controversial objectives. These objectives included a moratorium on executions and a new focus on procedural rights in death penalty cases. In other words, they opted to pursue nontransformative liberal democratic goals in a hostile political environment. As a result, they were able, as we noted in Chapter 2, to establish a "fragile and unstable" alliance with the organized legal profession (Sarat, 2001).

Finally, we come to emancipatory-democratic cause lawyering, which refocuses attention from the center of power to its periphery and from overarching democratic narratives to the empowerment of marginalized individuals in the family, the criminal and civil justice systems, the welfare office, and so forth.[14]

Emancipatory cause lawyers focus their energies on "micro-sites of power"—at localized and individualized instances of repression. In place of constitutional litigation or politicization, their primary tools include their forms of interaction with their clients, the organization of their practices, and vigorous representation of individual clients in whatever forums are appropriate—much in the manner of conventional legal practice (Trubek and Kransberger, 1998).

As one Seattle attorney put it, "My basic political beliefs are a kind of 'anti-ism' stance" (Scheingold, 1998: 134). As another lawyer explained,

I think it's also very important to empower people in their daily lives because I really believe that the way things change is not so much by impact litigation but by people feeling more sense of power in their daily lives, and being able to take more control and not being so downtrodden and powerless. I think our society does a lot to make people feel very powerless. . . . If you're gay it doesn't mean you have to commit suicide when you're twenty-one. There is a way to survive in society and you might be able to find one. A lot of these kids don't have any adult that they've been able to talk to about it. (Scheingold, 1998: 127, 134)

Those who adopt this "anti-ism" are in effect defining politics in personal terms and turning their backs on structural factors like class conflict and the power of the state and of corporations. Robert Fine and Sol Picciotto (1992: 6) make much the same point in connection with their account of *critical* cause lawyering. "Since the social relations between the classes are fragmented, the central antagonism takes the form of many *specific conflicts*, for example, over housing, the environment, racial and gender oppression."[15]

The transformative elements of social-democratic cause lawyering are embodied in the pursuit of second-generation rights to health care, housing, social security, a living wage, and the like. In more substantive terms, social democrats want to transform the state into an agent of equality—a welfare state rather than a liberal state. Emancipatory democracy aspires to a society and a polity which are participatory, nonhierarchical, and noncoercive. Yet it is not clear that the tactic of individual empowerment—so difficult to distinguish from conventional client representation—can serve transformative ends. In the final analysis, cause lawyers who confine themselves to such emancipatory projects may leave liberal democracy unreformed.[16]

Conclusion

While Tocqueville (1876) and Halliday (1998a) rightly call our attention to the contributions of lawyers to democracy, we must recognize that those contributions are enormously varied even among cause lawyers. Cause lawyering, like the American legal profession as a whole, is first and foremost a creature of, and a contributor to, liberal democracy. Cause lawyers who believe that first-generation rights are both the necessary and sufficient condition of democracy are unequivocally liberal. All three versions of liberal democratic cause lawyering—left-liberal, neoliberal, and libertarian—are wedded to rights which are embedded in the institutional and cultural foundation of the United States constitutional system. As a consequence, constitutional litigation tends to serve them well—although their fortunes vary as the political tides shift back and forth. They enjoy a satisfying and productive consonance between their aspirations and their legal resources, even when they do not prevail in meeting their immediate goals.

On the other hand, cause lawyers whose beliefs are at odds with liberal democracy face the daunting challenge of deploying the institutions and instruments of liberal democracy against itself (see Kinoy, 1983). Not surprisingly, those who challenge core premises of liberal democracy—irrespective of whether that challenge comes from the left or the right—are generally deprived of the opportunities afforded by constitutional litigation.[17] They are, therefore, much more dependent on various kinds of political mobilization (McCann and Silverstein, 1998).

Liberal democracy is, in the end, both a resource for and a constraint on cause lawyers. In their roles as lawyers it provides them distinctive institutions and instruments with which they can realize their beliefs and advance the causes they serve. But insofar as they remain faithful to their professional commitments, liberal democracy tames and domesticates them. It invites those with transformative aspirations to abandon their lawyering work; to face very high odds in continuing to use the tools of law or to trim their sails by making peace with the ends and means of liberal democracy. Insofar as they choose the third course, they can make some headway, but their victories may ring hollow. In effect, they legitimate the very institutions that they would like to dismantle, reminding us again that "the master's tools will never dismantle the master's house" (Lorde, 1984).

CHAPTER 6

Conclusion: Cause Lawyering in Comparative and Global Perspective

BY INSISTING on making a profession of their beliefs and on transforming ethics into political and moral advocacy, cause lawyers trouble traditional conceptions of lawyering and the institutions which support and reproduce them. They push the boundaries of the profession, seeking to overcome alienation with belief and to break down the barriers between vocation and commitment. Yet they maintain their identity as lawyers, remaining committed to the profession even as they challenge it, to law even as they pursue justice.

Justice, Drucilla Cornell (1990: 1697) argues, "is precisely what eludes our full knowledge." We cannot "grasp the Good but only follow it. The Good . . . is a star which beckons us to follow." While Justice, what Cornell (1988: 1587) calls the Good, is, on her account, always present *to* law; it is never completely realized *in* law. The law "posits an ideality . . . that it can never realize, and . . . this failure is constitutive of existing law" (Butler, 1990: 1716). Law exists both in the "as yet" failure to realize the Good and in the commitment to its realization. In this failure and this commitment, law is two things at once: a crucial mechanism for maintaining the social status quo, but also the arena to which citizens address themselves in the hope of improving society (see Young and Sarat, 1994).[1]

In a similar vein, Robert Cover (1983: 4) used the word *nomos*, "normative universe," to argue that law is crucially involved in helping persons "create and maintain a world of right and wrong, of lawful and unlawful, of valid and void." The *nomos* which law helps to create, Cover (1983: 9) believes, always contains within it visions of possibility not yet realized, conceptions of a better world not yet built.[2] However, Cover goes one step further. He reminds us that law is not simply, or even primarily, a gentle, hermeneutic apparatus. Law always exists in a state of tension between a world of meaning in which justice is pursued, and a world in which "legal interpretation takes place on a field of pain and death" (Cover, 1986: 1601).

Confronting this tension in law is the distinctive work of cause lawyers wherever they practice and whatever cause they serve. Cause lawyers use their professional skills to move law away from its daily reality and toward a vision of the Good. Cause lawyers use the skills and knowledge that they possess to give life to law's ethical aspirations. It is crucial to their professional identity "that they are morally accountable for their representation, not to be sure for promoting their clients' projects, but for advocating the political and legal principles they are trying to vindicate" (Luban, 1988: 161). Because they exemplify a legitimating ideal that indicates that lawyers can and should stand for something, cause lawyers are accommodated—albeit only conditionally—by a profession with a suspect reputation and tarnished public image. Because they are continually testing and transgressing boundaries, they are also resisted by, and within, institutions on which they depend.

Cause lawyers are both the voice of law's idealized self and irrefutable evidence of how and why that idealization is contested, never quite within reach and yet somehow infused into the law's meaning and processes (Sarat, 1998b: 318). They are, in other words, uniquely placed not simply to serve justice and democracy but to reformulate, and thus to destabilize, them. Because they are particularly sensitive to, and focused on, the shortcomings of liberal democracy and liberal legalism, they can and do often become intemperate and implacable critics of what *is* and creative voices of what can and therefore *should be*.

Of course, just like law, justice, and democracy, cause lawyers are not always all that they can be. They too are encumbered by the very institutions which empower them and must therefore make their peace with a less than perfect world. Still, their work requires that they continuously call attention to what ought to be done and to engage in activities which will contribute albeit haltingly and incrementally to ideals that are by definition elusive and never fully realized.

Each of the previous chapters in this book has examined an institution, or set of institutions, in which cause lawyering is both embedded and embattled: the bar, law schools, the sites of legal practice, and the political and legal agencies of American democracy. This book situates cause lawyering in relation to those institutions as they operate in the United States, emphasizing the opportunities they provide and the constraints they impose. In this chapter we first take stock of the lessons that can be gleaned from an examination of the situation of cause lawyering in the United States.

Second we relate those lessons to studies of cause lawyering elsewhere in the world. Those studies have focused primarily on the means and ends of cause lawyering rather than on its institutional contexts.[3] Yet research on cause lawyers outside the United States makes clear both the global reach of cause lawyering and its sensitivity to cultural, national, historical, and political variation. More specifically and perhaps most significantly, these findings reveal the many ways in which the story of cause lawyering today transcends the American experience. Finally, we examine cause lawyering's engagement with the worldwide process of globalization and the relevance of cause lawyering to the "state in a global era" (Sarat and Scheingold, 2001a).

The Institutionalization of Cause Lawyering in the United States: Opportunities and Constraints

The organized legal profession, law schools, legal practice, and political advocacy all provide the stages on which cause lawyering plays out in a drama of possibility and limitation. Cause lawyering rejects the orthodox conception of *legal professionalism* as the commodification of service excellence; of *legal education* as reducible to learning to think like a lawyer; of *legal practice* as client loyalty and income maximization; and of *public service* as civic professionalism and political neutrality. As a result, none of those institutions welcomes cause lawyering, but each of them—albeit to varying degrees and grudgingly—tolerates it. But given the ostensibly irreconcilable rejection of the interests and values driving conventional lawyering, why is there even grudging toleration? We argue that this toleration of cause lawyering is both a strategic calculation and the product of shared beliefs in lawyering as a cornerstone of state-society relations.

The Legal Profession

Within the organized legal profession, cause lawyering has been able to gain and maintain a foothold as a consequence of efforts made by the bar to protect the profession's own social capital. Earlier hostility to cause lawyering was an expression of the institutional interests of the legal profession—and specifically of its links to corporate wealth and its stake in social and professional stratification. Today the organized profession is no longer quite so hostile to cause lawyering. This is due to the profession's continuing efforts to enhance its public reputation by capitalizing on the public resonance of an inclusive understanding of rights and justice—ideals with which cause lawyering, but not the profession as a whole, is identified.

Cause lawyering has been, albeit to a limited extent, incorporated into the bar's definition of civic professionalism. While decidedly opportunistic, this accommodation to cause lawyering represents an acknowledgment not only of the profession's compact with the public but also of its own integrity and its constitutive links to the ideals of liberal democracy—including equal justice under law. In making room for cause lawyering, the legal profession protects its "democratic flank" (Auerbach, 1976: 16) and at the same time affirms its own responsibility for, and dependence upon, the values and institutions of liberal legality and liberal democracy.

It is, however, one thing to tolerate those versions of cause lawyering which serve liberal democratic rights and quite another to encourage and support cause lawyers whose goal is to transcend liberal democracy. The balance between professional opportunities and professional constraints shifts sharply in the latter direction insofar as cause lawyers, in pursuit of transformative agendas, destabilize taken-for-granted understandings of justice and democracy.

Legal Education

In legal education, even more than in the organized profession, cause lawyering—and not just cause lawyering on the political fringe—is marginalized. This is, however, more a result of indifference than confrontation. Resistance to cause lawyering is *implicit* in the core law school curriculum and especially in its pedagogy, which rewards cognitive and rhetorical skills and discourages moral and political advocacy. Administrators, faculty, and most students experience the expectations and values of would-be cause lawyers as threats to the status, the integrity, and the mission of the profession and to the role of legal education in serving the profession.

Cause lawyering is at once valorized in the hortatory rhetoric that seeks to explain what legal education contributes to society but is disregarded or disrespected in the day-to-day practices of law schools. As a result, the moral passion that many students bring to law school tends to be supplanted by what Robert Granfield (1992: 74) refers to as an "ideology of pragmatism." While there are currently programs, even entire law schools, dedicated to cause lawyering and designed to introduce its values and practices into the curriculum, the results of these efforts have so far at least not been encouraging.

Legal education is for most students a three-year retreat from causes and cause lawyering. However, some students do persist. This persistence is nurtured by extracurricular clinical projects that are associated with doing good. Because they provide law schools with a modicum of public service credibility and students with some practical experience, the place of these programs is secure even while their status remains low. Cause lawyering is also nurtured by subcultures of resistance within law schools. These subcultures develop within overtly political organizations linked to a variety of social movements. Thus law schools provide, albeit at the margins, and often in spite of themselves, a staging area for the production of cause lawyers.

Legal Practice

For cause lawyers, legal practice is replete with the kinds of opportunities and constraints that characterize the legal profession and legal education. For each cause lawyer, the search for "something to believe in" is a personal quest. In some cases, the objective is pragmatic and particular; causes are chosen without much reflection and with no ideological or programmatic strings attached. In other instances, commitment to a cause reflects serious dedication to a particular objective or to some broader ideal.

Cause lawyers gravitate to practice sites that are most consonant with their own priorities, and each site offers distinctive combinations of risk and reward.

- Pro bono programs in *corporate firms* provide the most limited reward while entailing fewest career risks. In return for a more than comfortable income, the time open for cause lawyering is very limited as are the choice of causes and the means to pursue them.
- *Salaried practice* constitutes a kind of moderate middle path. It assures full-time cause lawyering and a stable and adequate income. The agenda is, however, determined by the priorities of the organization.
- *Small-firm* cause lawyering is risky business: maximum freedom to choose causes, colleagues, tactics, and strategy, but in a setting that tends to be financially insecure, idiosyncratic, and volatile.

For some, the rewards of cause lawyering are insufficient and its burdens too heavy. Others thrive or at least persevere because of who they are and where they work, and because of the prevailing political and social ethos. Just as in the organized bar and in law school, the *costs* of cause lawyering both take their toll on and provide inspiration for the *practice* of cause lawyering.

Democratic Advocacy

To engage in democratic advocacy is to become embroiled in the ideological calculations which are the raison d'être of cause lawyering. The stakes in these calculations extend beyond individual career concerns to the collective import of cause lawyering as a democratic political institution. Insofar as cause lawyers in the United States are committed to liberal democracy, their choices are relatively painless. In effect, they risk relatively little, and the probability of reward is relatively high. On the other hand, insofar as cause lawyers find fault with liberal democracy and pursue transformative agendas, they are in effect playing a high-stakes game in which the risks are high and the probabilities of success are low.

Constitutional litigation, the bedrock of cause lawyering, provides institutional access, legitimacy, and bargaining leverage. All of these advantages are, however, most readily available in connection with liberal democratic objectives. Of course, liberal democracy is itself contested terrain, and the fortunes of liberal, neoliberal, and libertarian cause lawyers tend to wax and to wane along with changes in the political climate. However, it is fair to say that so long as cause lawyers work within the parameters of liberal democracy, they have the necessary access to make headway both legally and politically. While success in litigation and success in the political arena do not go hand in hand, the access that is available for liberal democratic cause lawyering has proved useful as a political resource for lawyers willing to move between legal and political arenas.

On the other hand, those who challenge core premises of liberal democracy—irrespective of whether that challenge comes from the left or the right—are generally deprived of the opportunities afforded by constitutional litigation. They therefore not only are much more dependent on political mobilization but must also mobilize *against* the law and *against* the grain of mainstream politics. This latter point must, however, be qualified. Mainstream conceptions have from time to time expanded beyond liberal democracy. This seems to be the case these days with respect to the religious right and was so earlier with respect to social democratic goals and values. As a rule, however, transformative cause lawyering faces the no-win choice of succumbing to the immediate but ultimately unsatisfactory rewards of liberal democracy or becoming, in effect, *lost-cause* lawyering (Sarat, 1998a).

Perspectives and Prospects: Beyond Liberal Democratic Regimes

All of these matters take on added meaning and portent when the focus shifts from cause lawyering, justice, and democracy in the United States to the infinitely more diverse and problematic world stage. Although research on cause lawyering outside the United States began in earnest only within the last decade, cause lawyering has been documented in Latin America, Western Europe, the Middle East, Southeast Asia, and Africa.[4]

Already there is ample evidence of the widespread institutionalization and persistence of cause lawyering. As we mentioned in Chapter 1, the spread of cause lawyering throughout the world can, in general, be traced to a number of structural factors. These include, in particular, an increase in written constitutions and constitutional courts, the neoliberal values driving globalization, and the development of transnational human rights networks (see, e.g., Dezalay and Garth, 2002).

While leaving no doubt that cause lawyering is, indeed, more likely to flourish in liberal democratic settings, research in settings outside the United States shows the important purposes it serves in other kinds of political regimes. Cause lawyering occurs in both autocratic and neocorporatist regimes—albeit with altered means, ends, and political salience. In autocratic and in dangerously unstable polities, even the pursuit of first-generation rights puts cause lawyering and cause lawyers in serious jeopardy. Certainly there are many states where to claim basic liberal rights is deemed a confrontational and hostile *political* act. Thus even the most modest forms of cause lawyering may be intolerable.

Not surprisingly, then, where liberal democracy is absent, achieving its values and norms becomes one of the overriding objectives of cause lawyers. Daniel Lev (1998) found this to be the case in Southeast Asia, where cause lawyering drew sustenance from within the legal profession with its commitment to rule of law. Richard Abel (1995) documents much the same kind of process in the efforts of cause lawyers in Apartheid South Africa to extend the protections and the opportunities provided by liberal democratic rights to blacks and coloreds who were effectively excluded from citizenship. Indeed, it can be argued that nowhere is cause lawyering more important than in regimes where even a rudimentary commitment to the rule of law is lacking.

A similar dynamic can be observed in Israel's neocorporatist democracy, with its racialized inflection of citizenship and the long-standing life-and-death conflict with the Palestinian-Arab "other." In this setting, proximity to the Israeli state and inclusion within the cohesive Israeli legal elite (Woods, forthcoming) are the best guarantors of effective cause lawyering. Israeli insiders tend to practice a collaborative form of cause lawyering and are generally reluctant to confront the state, particularly on matters of security (Dotan, 2001). Still, Palestinians, Bedouins, and other outsiders are not without legal recourse when their rights are violated (Hajjar, 2001; and Shamir and Chinsky, 1998). Rule-of-law institutions are in place, and some cause lawyers are willing to operate from beyond the corporatist compact. Others, working within that compact, oppose human rights abuses that are regarded as incompatible with their vision of Israeli democracy.

At the same time, the frustrations of cause lawyering in neocorporatist states that privilege consensual decision making and marginalize rights claiming lead to strategic adaptations which are analogous to those made by transformative lawyers in the United States. For example, Japanese cause lawyers, albeit with some reluctance, pursue politicization. They believe that success in the courtroom is likely to depend on demonstrating that their claims resonate in the polity. Accordingly, they have regularly, if reluctantly, taken on the onerous chore of organizing plaintiffs and helping them orchestrate campaigns to raise public consciousness and in this way to get the attention of the government (Kidder and Miyazawa, 1993; Miyazawa, 1996).

On the other hand, there seems to be a temptation in neocorporatist settings to take the law into one's own hands, so to speak. Thus, Ronen Shamir and Neta Ziv (2001: 287–93) identify a two-track strategy among lawyers working against Israel's land segregation policies. The legal track entailed antidiscrimination litigation on behalf of excluded Israeli Arabs by the Association for Civil Rights in Israel. At the same time "a parallel clandestine scheme" was undertaken to subvert land segregation policies. A willing Israeli surrogate was employed under "a covert agency agreement (a recognized device under Israel's Agency Law)" to purchase land on behalf of, and turn it over to, an Arab buyer. The clandestine track was arguably political rather than legal—"sub-politics" to use Shamir and Ziv's term—because the objective was not to vindicate law but to subvert it in order to advance values and an agenda to which the lawyers were themselves committed.

Despite its affinities with liberal democracy, the fewer the democratic alternatives, the more vital cause lawyering becomes. Cause lawyering has proved itself surprisingly adaptable to ostensibly hostile settings. These adaptations are different from, but analogous to, those which we have documented in the United States as cause lawyers accommodate variation in the political climate and among practice sites and pursue political visions which challenge liberal democracy.

Perspectives and Prospects: Globalization and Transnational Advocacy

Just as the formation of nation-states was one of the defining characteristics of an earlier era, their rapid and often radical transformation is one of the defining characteristics of ours. Under pressures variously labeled transnationalism and globalization, state forms throughout the world alter and adapt, adding new functions, shedding old ones, refining institutional processes, developing new alliances within and beyond national borders, sometimes increasing democratic tendencies, sometimes weakening them. In response to those pressures and the alterations and adaptations of states, local and subnational forces assert themselves, sometimes challenging the state, sometimes working with and within it.

In this era, state power flows outward *via globalization* to transnational forces and institutions, and it flows inward *via democratization* to subnational institutions and social movements. Both bring new pressures to bear on, and complicate, state action. Both play out in different ways in different nations and in the different arenas of the state. Independently and in combination with one another, democratization and globalization confront cause lawyers with new issues and new burdens while altering their resources and their tactical and strategic options.

To an important extent globalization and at least one form of state transformation, namely democratization, work in tandem—encroaching on state power from above (globalization) and from below (democratization), but that is only one part of the story. Globalization may, in some circumstances, promote democratization, but only a rather limited form of democracy. Accordingly, advocates of democratization often find globalization more of a problem than a solution.

Additionally, to the extent that globalization does foster democratic transformations of states and greater democratization in already democratic states, it is as an incidental by-product rather than as an intended consequence. This is because globalization is driven by, and gives priority to, the economic rationality of corporate capitalism. Despite some convergence, then, democratization and globalization follow different trajectories and are at least as likely to work at cross-purposes as to be mutually reinforcing. They may push cause lawyers in different directions, the one creating opportunities and possibilities as the other poses obstacles and imposes barriers.

The hallmark of globalization as it is generally understood today is the worldwide spread of corporate capitalism and neoliberal values (Chase-Dunn, 1991). In other words, globalization should not be equated with the construction of an open, apolitical, and beneficent global village (Jameson, 1998). Instead, it is first and foremost a vast project in political economy that is restructuring the global order in ways that maximize its compatibility with the values and interests of multinational corporate enterprise and reorient dominant political ideologies. The mission of institutional messengers of globalized capitalism is to dismantle barriers to the free flow of populations, commerce, information, and especially capital—all in the service of economic growth and industrial development.

States respond in a variety of ways to the pressures of globalization—developing new governing ideologies, increasing some commitments while backing away from others, rearranging institutional forms, and so on. But state transformation is not a one-way street. Each state has its own distinctive character, structure, ideology, and trajectory—all the products of deeply embedded historical, cultural, and material factors.

One of the most important dimensions of state transformation in a global era is democratization. One indicator of this development is the fact that democracy, at least in the formal, procedural sense, has in recent years been gaining ground in many modernizing states. The so-called third wave (Huntington, 1991) of emergent democratic institutions has been spearheaded first by the collapse of communist regimes in Eastern and Central Europe, with the collateral discrediting of Marxist-Leninist approaches to modernization. More recently, the Asian economic crisis discredited the authoritarian capitalism of that region. Modernizing states around the world are now, with varying degrees of enthusiasm, pursuing neoliberal paths to economic expansion. In the political realm, this has often but not always meant, as Dietrich Rueschemeyer and his colleagues have pointed out, the introduction of "free and fair elections of representatives with universal and equal suffrage." Finally, states have acknowledged the importance of "the freedoms of expression and association as well as the protection of individual rights against arbitrary state action" (Rueschemeyer, Stephens, and Stephens, 1992: 45).

In so-called advanced capitalist societies, basic democratic institutions are well entrenched but coming under increasing pressure. To begin with, a deterioration of civil society is signaled by declining rates of participation in elections and in civic and political associations—all, some would say, indicative of a civil society losing its vigor (Putnam, 1995, 1996). In addition, the encroachment of the state on civil society is threatening its autonomy (Cohen, 1987; Rose, 1996a, 1996b, 1999; Donzelot, 1979).

A number of other structural problems are also plaguing advanced capitalist states. The very scale of government seems to overwhelm efforts at democratic management (Habermas, 1986). So too do the "contradictions of the welfare state," which pit the preconditions for economic growth against the fiscal resources required for inclusive forms of social and economic citizenship (Offe, 1984). As a consequence, a certain paralysis of democratic institutions has been detected and with it an inability to adequately confront the complex and divisive problems facing advanced capitalist societies (Garland, 1996; Lowi, 1979).

As these global forces impinge on the state, cause lawyering itself is transformed. Cause lawyers become engaged in new local contests over global economic and political developments. As states take on new forms and new values, new possibilities for working within, as well as against, the state open up (see Shamir, 1998). Moreover, in a global political economy, cause lawyering itself can be and is being globalized. New networks and connections emerge; new resources for sharing information and obtaining advice open up. Lawyering no longer can be contained by or within national boundaries (Halliday, 1998b).

Yet efforts by cause lawyers to take advantage of these changes embroil them in controversies: Are they being co-opted by corporate capitalism? Do the international institutions of globalization serve primarily to advance Western interests and ideas, thus promoting neoimperialism and neocolonialism? In response, can cause lawyers develop new strategies of legitimation?

For cause lawyers, what this means is that globalization and state transformation may be a mixed blessing. In some contexts it provides a political structure wherein minimal rights claims and legal defenses against abuses of state power become meaningful. In other contexts, it erodes support for the kinds of social changes which these lawyers, and the movements with which they are affiliated, seek to advance.

In modernizing societies, where democratic institutions are rudimentary and fragile, the issue becomes whether and how cause lawyering itself plays a role in the process of converting the contradictions of capitalism into opportunities for democratic transformation. In liberal democratic states, cause lawyering is in a much more favorable and secure position than in settings where modernization is still a work in progress (Sarat and Scheingold, 2001b). Yet even in advanced capitalist societies, the position of cause lawyers has in recent decades grown more problematic. Long established social, economic, and legal rights are under pressure (Simon, 1997; and Garland, 1996). Cause lawyers face the dual burden of greater need and dwindling resources, which occur with the triumph of neoliberalism.

Paralleling globalization as a factor in the transformation of states, while softening some of its insistent economic imperatives, are newly emergent international and supranational human rights regimes.[5] Today governments everywhere claim to believe in and respect the dignity of their citizens (Teson, 1985; Parekh, 1993). As a result, the *language* of human rights, if not human rights themselves, is nearly universal (Weissbrodt, 1989). "The past few decades," Richard Wilson (1996: 1) notes, "have witnessed the inexorable rise of the application of international human rights law as well as the extension of a wider public discourse on human rights, to the point where human rights could be seen as one of the most globalized political values of our times."

Human rights can be a source of both empowerment and protection for persons against the societies in which they live, or they can constrain those same persons (Merry, 1995; Sarat and Kearns, 2001). Human rights can liberate or limit the imagination of the possible; they can revolutionize or conserve. Like all rights, international human rights both authorize action and undermine authority's claims.

This is all enormously significant for cause lawyers who seek to deploy human rights norms locally to mobilize social movements or to legitimate particular demands (Collier, 2001). With or without recourse to transnational networks, they can pursue democratization and the vindication of human rights through confrontations with central institutions of the state. These confrontations occur by way of test case litigation—both national and supranational—as well as by leveraging the threat of litigation to force political concessions. But cause lawyers also work to exploit the fragmentation of state institutions (Scheingold, 1998; see also Fine and Picciotto, 1992). In short, democratization and human rights are produced, in part, by the activities of cause lawyers as they emerge in both national and transnational social movements.

The success of transnational cause lawyering appears, however, to correlate directly with the extent to which an indigenous presence is established. Thus there are several well-researched instances in which "imported" cause lawyers failed in their work as a consequence of unrealistic expectations derived from assumptions based on the U.S. model and the inability or unwillingness to adapt to the local scene.

- Noga Morag-Levine (2001) discovered that the efforts in Israel of U.S.-backed and -trained environmental lawyers to engage in adversarial legalism were on balance distrusted. This was due both to their American origins and to a more general hostility toward an abstract and aggressive legal rights campaign out of touch with Israeli political values and practices.

- Also in Israel, Ronen Shamir and Sara Chinsky (1998) discovered that U.S.-trained cause lawyers with ambitious goals derived from the U.S. experience found themselves unable to cope with the day-to-day frustrations of working on behalf of dispossessed Bedouins.

- Lucie White's (2001) research in Ghana also reveals how and why transnational networks become obstacles to the development of indigenous connections. More specifically, she finds that these networks tend to subordinate welfare claims to an access-to-justice agenda that is more compatible with the neoliberal values of economic development than with the needs of dispossessed Ghanaians.

- Anne Bloom (2001) discovered that personal injury lawyers proved to be unreliable advocates for workers employed by U.S. corporations in their factories located outside the country. They showed very little interest in mobilizing transnational networks, and they subordinated the clients' cause to their own efforts to ward off the threat posed by tort reform to their highly remunerative asbestos litigation.

Conversely, Stephen Meilli's (2001) research in Latin America reveals the growth of transnational networks that bring together cause lawyers working at the grass roots on behalf of both liberal and social democratic agendas. In short, the transnational opportunities afforded by globalization are more likely to be realized if they are localized—"community oriented and place oriented" (Shamir and Ziv, 2001: 298; and Coutin, 2001).

There is certainly evidence that cause lawyers are participating in and influencing the transformation of the state by contributing both to the construction of new global arrangements and to grassroots empowerment. Yet results vary significantly from place to place, and everywhere the challenges facing cause lawyers are enormous.

Conclusion

Cause lawyering in the United States and elsewhere is in constant transition as it seeks to adjust to changing configurations of state power. These transitions relate to the strategy, tactics, recruitment, reproduction, and organization of cause lawyers—as well as to relationships between cause lawyers and mainstream professionals. New opportunities are matched by new constraints. The already complex world of cause lawyering is further complicated by the webs of possibilities and barriers associated with the contemporary multiplication of legal spaces at national and transnational levels; with disaggregating, loosely coupled state structures, proliferating networks of activists, lawyers, and nongovernmental organizations; and with new ideological configurations.

For cause lawyers, globalization and state transformation emerge as a mixed blessing. In some contexts they provide a political structure wherein minimal rights claims and legal defenses against abuses of state power become meaningful. In other contexts, they erode support for the kinds of social changes which cause lawyers, and the movements with which they are affiliated, seek to advance.

How, why, and to what extent cause lawyers are taking effective advantage of the multiple opportunities made available to them within the United States and around the world remain open issues. We know a fair amount about how political context influences chances for success. On the other hand, we know very little about how variations in the organized profession, legal education, and legal practice influence the opportunities available to cause lawyers beyond the United States. After all, the distinctive social and professional contributions of cause lawyering flow directly from, and are made possible by, its structural engagement with the profession, the legal academy, and conventional legal practice.[6] If, therefore, we are to understand cause lawyering as a global undertaking, it is essential that our research agenda extend to the institutional contexts which have proved so revealing of cause lawyering in the United States. Similarly, the available research on globalization provides only a glimpse of its impact on cause lawyering and vice versa.

Just as justice has a contingent relationship to law, so cause lawyering has, and will have, a contingent relationship to conventional legal practice and to mainstream professional organization.

Even as cause lawyers in the United States work within the tensions described in this book, the world pushes in on them and draws them beyond our borders. Beyond as well as within the United States, cause lawyering emerges as a constitutive voice of law's idealized vision and its institutionalized practices. The world is, for the foreseeable future, the new stage on which cause lawyers will pursue the project of making a profession of their beliefs, and the future of democracy and globalization depends, in no small measure, on their success in doing so.

Notes

1. We are grateful to Tanina Rostain for calling this fact to our attention.

2. There are exceptions, most notably members of the plaintiffs' bar associated with the Trial Lawyers for Public Justice. These lawyers, like some in the criminal defense bar, share a mix of moral commitment and market incentives that do not permit their easy categorization as conventional lawyers.

3. The substantial and revealing dispute about whether there was a golden age for the U.S. legal profession—and, if so, when it occurred—is considered in Chapter 2.

4. This is not the place for a complete account of Parsons's view of the law, but perhaps one can get the functional flavor of the enterprise and of law's roles from a simple listing of the four contributions that he sees law making to the mitigation of social conflict. Law has the capacity to enhance *legitimization*, to clarify *meaning*, to impose *sanctions*, and to locate *authority* (Parsons, 1962: 58–59). Parsons also argues that the more deep-seated the social conflict, the less effective is law at resolving conflict. "Law flourishes particularly in a society in which most fundamental questions of social values are not currently at issue or under agitation. If there is sufficiently acute value conflict, law is likely to go by the board" (Parsons, 1962: 71). On "law as an integrative mechanism," see also Harry Bredemeier's article (1962) in the same volume.

5. Parsons (1962: 67) sees the lawyer in part as offering "relief from anxiety"—making, in other words, a "psychotherapeutic" intervention. "In order to be capable, psychologically, of 'getting things off his chest' a person must be assured that, within certain limits . . . sanctions will not operate. . . . The confidential character of the lawyer's relation to his client provides such a situation. The client can talk freely, to an understanding and knowledgeable ear, without fear of immediate repercussions."

6. It is suggestive that Parsons's functionalism was the prevailing sociological paradigm in the 1950s. This is the period when Glendon went to law school, when she began to practice law and the period which she identifies as the golden era of legal practice. It was also, she acknowledges (1994: 28), "a time of shameless exclusionary practices"—and, one might add, not only in the legal profession.

7. Luban (1988) makes a case for why it is ethically appropriate—indeed praiseworthy—for lawyers to serve broader visions of justice. He is also clearly aware of the practical and principled pitfalls of doing so. He addresses these pitfalls and offers guidelines for how to avoid them. For our purposes, the adequacy of his guidelines is less important than are the ethical tensions revealed by his analysis of the refocusing of representation from client to cause.

8. While we emphasize the principled element of the choice between legal and political engagement, that choice is also driven by instrumental considerations, as we make clear in Chapter 4.

9. Even in settings which are not liberal democratic, the pursuit of rights may well prove professionally acceptable, and although politically precarious, even dangerous, not necessarily out of the question. There is evidence in support of this proposition from apartheid South Africa (Abel, 1995), neocorporatist Japan (Kidder and Miyazawa, 1993), and Israel (Hajjar, 1997), as well as an essentially authoritarian setting like Indonesia (Lev, 1998).

CHAPTER 2

1. We hope to keep in tension a focus on the bar's ongoing ethical commitments and its legitimation needs. Both are, in our view, necessary to explain resistance and accommodations in its relation to cause lawyering.

2. Abel and Lewis's (1989) project on lawyers in both the common and civil law systems affirmed this function of professionalism as economic monopoly. Halliday and Karpik (1997: 3) also call attention to the synergy between the ostensibly competing conceptions of professionalism as expertise and market control, respectively. They point out that control of professional

knowledge is a way of "seizing and holding 'jurisdictions' of work"—thus reinforcing control of the market.

3. For a vigorous defense of the hired-gun theory see Freedman, 1975.

4. Scholars for whom this era of civic professionalism is inseparable from other goals contest Auerbach's vision. "In the early nineteenth century," Gordon (1988: 41) observes, "law practice for its leading practitioners was plainly instrumental (and often indeed incidental) to other goals. It provided the social contacts, the location in a center of political and commercial networks, and financing, for engagement in public life. . . . To a large extent, public activity was instrumental to their private ambitions."

5. Note in this connection that the following provision of the ABA's 1969 *Model Code of Professional Responsibility* (1980) was not included in the current *Model Rules of Professional Conduct* (2003). "A person or organization that pays or furnishes lawyers to represent others . . . may be interested in furthering their own economic, political, or social goals without regard to the responsibility of the lawyer to the individual client. . . . Since a lawyer must always be free to exercise his professional judgments without a third person, the lawyer who is employed by one to represent another must constantly guard against the erosion of his professional freedom" (Canon 5: EC 5–23, p. 40). This change presumably represents an implicit recognition by the ABA of the permeable character of the once bright ethical line dividing the legal from the political, the economic, and the social.

CHAPTER 3

1. "Public interest" lawyering was the subject of the research we will be discussing in this chapter. We have, however, taken the liberty of substituting our term, *cause lawyering*. We believe, for reasons discussed in Chapter 1, that we can do so without doing violence to the findings of the researchers or the sentiments of the law students.

2. While it is important to acknowledge that virtually all of this research was conducted over a limited period of time in the 1970s and 1980s, and at only a handful of the U.S. law schools, its basic message is both consistent and unchallenged.

3. Goodrich (1991: 3), it should be noted, was not "a typical first-year; I was a freelance legal reporter on a one-year fellowship," who did nonetheless take the standard array of first-year courses. Somewhat paradoxically, he notes that his "experience at Yale proved to be among the most rewarding in my life, but I remain thankful, nonetheless, that I decided against law years earlier."

4. All of these commentators seem to critique legal education from the political left. However, as we noted earlier, Kennedy's conservative colleague, Mary Ann Glendon, also seems to believe that legal education tends to have a pernicious impact on law students.

5. The career implications of all this are predictable and help explain why it is that students can believe that they are more political, more inclined toward pro bono work, and less interested in cause lawyering. On the one hand, given a more complex and pragmatic perspective, corporations and corporate practice become more acceptable. On the other hand, it becomes increasingly clear that legal advocacy is not a very reliable means of correcting social injustice. One of the problems is resources: "I worked . . . for a three-month clinical and I just realized that you can do only so much because they have so few resources. I decided that 'private' public interest jobs were the best of all possible worlds" (Granfield, 1992: 90). It follows that a bit of rights advocacy via pro bono work allows one to use the resources available in corporate firms to do the job in a professionally respectable fashion.

6. Scott Cummings (2004: 22–27) explores the roots of this tension between pro bono lawyering and cause lawyering. He provides a thoughtful analysis of how that tension plays out in the world of legal practice. We will return to this issue in Chapter 4.

7. Recall our discussion of legal realism in Chapter 2 and, in particular, of Laura Kalman's finding (1996: 16): "Where traditional law professors exalted legal doctrine, realists spoke of 'integrating' law with political science, economics, anthropology, sociology, and linguistics."

8. Kennedy (1982) makes much the same point, but more subversively so. His argument is that the pedagogy of immersion (our term) is part of the broader scheme of preparing students for the hierarchy of corporate practice. Insofar as the faculty makes it as difficult as possible to learn, the brightest, the most persistent, and the most deferential students will rise to the top of the class. At one and the same time, therefore, students are ranked for purposes of recruitment and made compliant for the daily grind of corporate practice.

9. Granfield (1992: 81) argues that students collude with the faculty on these matters. The faculty makes it clear that those who "make moral arguments on the basis of equity or social justice are considered intellectually soft," and they are then "ridiculed by the other students." As one student put it, "It's hard to be a talker here. I found out that I was on the turkey bingo list and I was appalled. The resentment of me . . . was strong . . . people in the corridors . . . would snub me." Being dubbed a turkey, Granfield explains, is based both on being too serious about the law and too committed to an ideological position.

10. We are grateful to Tanina Rostain for suggesting this point.

11. Faculty members participating in public interest and clinical programs have called our attention to a recent increase in just the kinds of activities that may provide sustenance to would-be cause lawyers. While we were unable to find published research on how these programs are structured or on how extensive they are, a Google search revealed a host of public interest activities at a diverse collection of law schools—including, for example, Brooklyn, Columbia, Delaware, Denver, Dickinson, Harvard, New England, New College of California, Rutgers, Santa Clara, Stanford, Tennessee, UCLA, Villanova, and Wisconsin.

CHAPTER 4

1. Joel Handler, Ellen Jane Hollingsworth, and Howard Erlanger (1978: 180) discovered more than two decades ago that legal rights activities created structured opportunities and generated inertial forces that maintained involvement in legal rights over the long haul and beyond a particular job. They found, for example, that pro bono work performed by *former* poverty lawyers in private practice "was greater in quantity and more oriented toward social reform than the norm of the bar." (See also Kilwein, 1998). Carrie Menkel-Meadow (1998: 41) refers to the process that activates and sustains cause lawyering as "mixed-motive altruism." Ronen Shamir and Sara Chinsky's (1998) research on attorneys for the Bedouins in Israel demonstrates that the process of representation can itself—even without initial altruistic impulses—construct causes and, indeed, cause lawyers.

2. We use the terms *practice site* and *professional venue* to identify the lawyer's place of professional employment—her or his day job, so to speak. We thus distinguish where lawyers are employed from their site (or sites) of advocacy—trial courts, appellate courts, regulatory agencies, and so forth (cf. Krishnan, forthcoming).

3. For a politically salient illustration of these patterns, consider how an increasingly conservative political ethos has constrained the career options for left-wing cause lawyers while giving rise to a thriving cadre of right-wing cause lawyers.

4. Consider, for example, the Seattle-King County Bar Association's city-wide network of free neighborhood legal clinics staffed by volunteer attorneys. These clinics have no income qualifications and are confined to giving advice rather than taking on clients. Normally this amounts to brief encounters with a working- or middle-class constituency. The attorneys are not further obligated. They need not engage emotionally with their "clients"—nor will the attorneys in such programs connect to the broader issues of democ-

racy, social justice, and marginalization through contact with the "truly dis-advantaged." Insofar as firms encourage associates to participate exclusively or primarily in such clinics, they are being steered toward a conception of unmet needs that falls short of robust cause lawyering (Scheingold and Bloom, 1998).

5. Young litigators also have more self-serving motivations for engaging in pro bono programs, where they can gain valuable experience, substantial notoriety, a sense of professional efficacy, and direct access to real clients—none of which tends to be otherwise available to them.

6. Cause lawyers often work hours as long and as intense as those worked in corporate firms. However, they work because of their commitment, not to satisfy an organization's need to generate revenue.

7. The struggle to reconcile these two different objectives has also been the source of internal friction within the program. On one side were the obscure attorneys in the foxholes of the legal war on poverty. They were charged with the Sisyphean task of client service, which could address only the indicia of poverty. On the other side were their more celebrated coworkers engaged in ambitious strategies against the structural sources of poverty (Katz, 1982).

8. According to *The New Yorker* (Bowe, 2003), the CIW is funded from five-dollar membership fees. What is unclear from the article is how the Florida Legal Services attorneys managed to circumvent legal services' restrictive client representation rules. The most likely explanation is that the Florida program, as was the case elsewhere in the country, gave up federal funding in order to pursue a more satisfying cause lawyering agenda.

9. Susan Coutin (2001) and Michael McCann (1994) discovered an analogous sense of identification with, and loyalty to, the immigration and labor organizations which they researched.

10. Available research does not distinguish between solo practitioners and small firms, even though it is reasonable to believe the risk and reward calculations differ at the two practice sites.

CHAPTER 5

1. This kind of evolution can be detected, and will be discussed below, in the lives of cause lawyers who identify with the transformative left.

2. According to Santos (1995: 407), inequality inheres in the exercise of power, which is inevitably constituted by "any social relation ruled by an unequal exchange." Emancipation, therefore, cannot be achieved through regulation but only through dialogue and persuasion which purge power from democracy. In addition, there must be multiple versions of emancipa-

tory knowledge suitable to each of the innumerable "clusters of social relations" (Santos, 1995: 441) constituting political society.

3. As for third-generation rights, we see emancipatory democracy as embracing their utopian spirit and to some extent their specific aspirations to peace, security, a healthy environment, safe natural resources, and group self-determination.

4. Laura Hatcher (forthcoming) traces the emergence of neoliberal cause lawyering to the 1970s and, specifically, to the National Legal Center for the Public Interest (NLCPI). She argues that the NLCPI was "instrumental in establishing a group of public interest law foundations throughout the United States including organizations such as the Mountain States Legal Foundation and the Southeastern Legal Foundation."

5. Indeed Hatcher (forthcoming: 22) argues that its founders created the Institute for Justice (in her words) "out of growing concern that other conservatives were not working hard enough to protect economic liberties."

6. The spirit of this claim is captured by the "campaign" hyperbole of a candidate for the ACLU State Board in Washington: "Civil liberties is my religion; the ACLU is my church."

7. This attorney derives satisfaction from demonstrating to his "astonished" clients that a "lawyer" can "help them do something and get some results" (Scheingold and Bloom, 1998: 230).

8. Note that these categories are in practice more fluid than our summary suggests. Ann Southworth (forthcoming: 30), for example, reports that a "lawyer who works for a Christian evangelical group began prosecuting pornography cases to gain trial experience; 'I wasn't particularly religious. . . . I got into these cases, not because I had a passion for the work, but because I just wanted the jury trials.' At first, he was repelled by some of the evangelical Christians associated with the fight against pornography, but years later, after he had become a well-known pornography prosecutor, he became an evangelical Christian himself." Further muddying the waters is the participation of Catholic organizations in the evangelical campaign against abortion.

9. Consider the preamble to the NLG constitution: "The National Lawyers Guild is an association dedicated to the need for basic change in the structure of our political and economic system. We seek to unite the lawyers, law students, legal workers, and jail house lawyers of America in an organization which shall function as an effective political and social force in the service of the people, to the ends that human rights shall be regarded as more sacred than property interests" (Rabinowitz and Ledwith, 1987: back cover). In its early years, the Guild was more liberal and reformist, with an emphasis on extending rights via an approach to precedent redolent of the

legal realism that was so influential in the 1930s. Thus, the preamble to the Guild's original 1937 constitution does *not* mention the need for "basic change in the structure of our political and economic system" or for lawyers as "an effective political and social force" (Ginger and Tobin, 1988: 11). Clearly, the Guild has adopted a much more transformative position in recent decades.

10. One need not be a doctrinaire socialist to miss socialism as a unifying ideal—however vaguely defined. See, for example, Norman Rush's (1994) lament, "What Was Socialism and Why We Will All Miss It So Much."

11. One of the earliest and ultimately unsuccessful transformative efforts was the attempt in the 1970s by the National Welfare Rights Organization (NWRO) to convert the welfare system in the United States from a mechanism for "regulating the poor" (Piven and Cloward, 1972) into an agent of egalitarian redistribution. While the legal campaign did lead to due process protections for welfare recipients, it did not prove possible to leverage litigation and political action to provide a social-democratic alternative to welfare. Indeed, the campaign did not even allow the NWRO to maintain its role as a player in the politics of welfare (Scheingold, 1974: 139–40).

12. There are many other instances of cause lawyers engaging in political mobilization on behalf of animal rights (Silverstein, 1996), immigrants (Coutin, 2001), tenant unions (Kelly, 1994: 157), Act Up (Scheingold, 1998: 136).

13. Ironically, confirmation of the transformative potential of civil litigation is provided by the concerted campaign waged by neoliberals against the trial lawyers (Haltom and McCann, forthcoming). However, Anne Bloom's research (2001) on the use of civil litigation to force American corporations to improve the conditions of their workers in foreign countries reveals that individual trial lawyers are often more interested in protecting their social capital than in politicizing, or even in pursuing, causes. Similarly, while candidate John Edwards did not disavow his reputation as a trial lawyer, neither did he make those civil justice successes a centerpiece of his populist campaign—thus suggesting that the tide of tort reform has yet to turn.

14. Emancipatory democracy, as we have suggested earlier, is infused with the visionary *spirit* of third-generation rights—although there is only a partial correlation with the *letter* of third-generation rights.

15. Strictly speaking, the anti-ism stance of practicing cause lawyers goes only a portion of the way toward Santos's (1995) vision of emancipatory democracy in that they continue to work through and depend upon formal legal institutions. Still, in their turn from "politics writ large," their local focus, and their efforts to empower individuals to resist the state, they partake

in the spirit of, and can reasonably be seen as a practical step toward, emancipatory democracy.

16. To some extent, then, we agree with an anonymous reviewer of an earlier version of this book who pointed out that *in practice* critical lawyering is, at best, a poor example of what Santos (1995) might recognize as emancipatory cause lawyering. *In principle*, however, the ideals expressed in the critical lawyering literature resonate well with Santos's emancipatory aspirations (see Grigg-Spall and Ireland, 1992).

17. Arguably, there is an exception to these generalizations about transformative lawyering—and indeed about the shared plight of the transformative-right and the transformative-left. The secular tilt of the American constitutional system notwithstanding, evangelical cause lawyers seem to have both constitutional and cultural leverage that is today largely unavailable to the transformative-left. In the United States the relationship of state and society to religion has always been marked by a kind of benevolent ambivalence. Religious symbols and values have been continuously prominent in American public life. We are fond of describing ourselves as a God-fearing nation. School prayers were widely accepted and went unchallenged until the middle of the twentieth century. Prayers are still heard in Congress—led by chaplains who are government employees. We emboss our trust in God on coins. The list could go on and on. It could, for example, be reasonably argued, and evangelical cause lawyers regularly do, that the First Amendment's proscription of an established religion is more about a nonsectarian than about a secular state. As a consequence, evangelical-democratic cause lawyers seem to have access to constitutional discourse. To be sure, they lose some and they win some, but so long as they confine themselves to nonsectarian arguments, they have reason to believe that they will give as good as they get.

CHAPTER 6

1. "Law is simultaneously a denial of the ethical in the name of the political and a denial of the political in the name of the ethical" (Young and Sarat, 1994: 326).

2. Cover (1983: 9) elaborates as follows: "Law may be viewed as a system of tension or a bridge linking a concept of reality to an imagined alternative. . . . Thus, one constitutive element of a *nomos* is the phenomenon George Steiner has labeled 'alternity': the 'other than the case,' the counterfactual propositions, images, shapes of will and evasions with which we charge our mental being and by means of which we build the changing, largely fictive milieu for our somatic and our social existence. But the concept of a *nomos* is

not exhausted by its 'alternity'; it is neither utopia nor pure vision. A *nomos*, as a world of law, entails the application of human will to an extant state of affairs as well as toward our visions of alternative futures."

3. Consequently legal education has been largely disregarded, and historical and professional matters have been given only subsidiary attention.

4. We are confident that there is much as yet "undocumented" cause lawyering going on in these areas as well as elsewhere.

5. As we see them, international and supranational human rights are not themselves necessary consequences of economic globalization. Given their institutional trajectories and their ideological foundations, we believe it is important to see globalization and human rights regimes as separate and distinct from one another. While there are affinities and even alliances, they march to very different drummers: globalization to requisite worldwide capitalism and human rights to moral principle.

6. For example, there is reason to believe that one of the reasons that it is easier to engage in cause lawyering in the United States is because there are multiple sources of financial support: government funding, pro bono programs, and a multiplicity of social advocacy organizations. Some, but not all, of these funding sources are available elsewhere, for example, in the United Kingdom. In contrast, Japanese cause lawyers rely entirely on monies diverted by small firms from paying clients to causes. Not only does this put a heavy burden on the firms themselves, but it also means that Japanese cause lawyers have an interest in restricting the ranks of the legal profession—despite a widely recognized shortage of lawyers. While expanding the number of lawyers would increase access to justice, it might well hurt cause lawyering by leading to lower fees and a greater reluctance to redistribute them.

References

Abbott, Anthony. 1988. *The System of Professions: An Essay on the Division of Expert Labor.* Chicago: University of Chicago Press.

Abel, Richard. 1981. "Why Does the American Bar Association Promulgate Ethical Rules?" *Texas Law Review* 59: 639.

———. 1987. "Lawyers." In *Law and the Social Sciences*, ed. Leon Lipson and Stanton Wheeler. New York: Russell Sage.

———. 1995. *Politics by Other Means: Law in the Struggle Against Apartheid, 1980–1994.* New York: Routledge.

———. 2002. "Choosing, Nurturing, Training, and Placing Public Interest Law Students." *Fordham Law Review* 70: 1563.

Abel, Richard, and P. S. Lewis. 1989. *Lawyers in Society*, 3 vols. Berkeley: University of California Press, 1989.

American Bar Association. 1980. *Model Code of Professional Responsibility.* Adopted 1969 by the House of Delegates, amended 1970, 1974, 1975, 1976, 1977, 1978, and 1980 (PDF file).

———. 1997. "Resolution of the House of Delegates" and "Report Accompanying Resolution." (February 3.)

———. 2003. *Model Rules of Professional Conduct.* Chicago: Center for Professional Responsibility.

American Bar Association Commission on Professionalism. 1986. *"In the Spirit of Public Service": A Blueprint for the Rekindling of Lawyer Professionalism.*

Amsterdam, Anthony. 1998. "Selling a Quick Fix for Boot Hill: The Myth of Justice Delayed in Death Cases." In *The Killing State: Capital Punishment in*

Law, Politics, and Culture, ed. Austin Sarat. New York: Oxford University Press.

Auerbach, Jerold S. 1976. *Unequal Justice: Lawyers and Social Change in Modern America*. New York: Oxford University Press.

Bachmann, Steve. 1984–85. "Lawyers, Law, and Social Change." *New York University Review of Law and Social Change* 13: 1.

Ball, Terrence, and Richard Dagger. 1995. *Political Ideologies and the Democratic Ideal*, 2nd ed. New York: HarperCollins.

Barber, Benjamin. 1984. *Strong Democracy*. Berkeley: University of California Press.

Barclay, Scott, and Anna-Maria Marshall. Forthcoming. "Supporting a Cause, Developing a Movement, and Consolidating a Practice: Cause Lawyers and Sexual Orientation Litigation in Vermont." In *The Worlds Cause Lawyers Make: Structure and Agency in Legal Practice*, ed. Austin Sarat and Stuart A. Scheingold. Stanford, CA: Stanford University Press.

Bell, Derrick. 1976. "Serving Two Masters: Integration Ideals and Client Interests in School Desegregation Litigation." *Yale Law Journal* 85: 470.

Berkman, Harvey. 1995. "Costs Mount for Indigent Defense." *National Law Journal*, August 7, A18.

Berlin, Isaiah. 1958. *Two Concepts of Liberty*. Oxford: Clarendon Press.

Bloom, Anne. 2001. "Taking on Goliath: Why Personal Injury Litigation May Represent the Future of Transnational Cause Lawyering." In *Cause Lawyering and the State in a Global Era*, ed. Austin Sarat and Stuart Scheingold. New York: Oxford University Press.

Boaz, David. 1997. *Libertarianism: A Primer*. New York: Free Press.

Bowe, John. 2003. "Nobodies: Does Slavery Exist in America?" *The New Yorker*, April 21 and 28: 106.

Brandeis, Louis. 1933. "The Opportunity in Law." In *Business—A Profession*. Boston: Hale, Cushman and Flint.

Bredemeier, Harry C. 1962. "Law as an Integrative Mechanism." In *Law and Sociology: Exploratory Essays*, ed. William M. Evan. New York: Free Press of Glencoe.

Brown, Steven. 2002. *Trumping Religion: The New Christian Right, the Free Speech Clause, and the Courts*. Tuscaloosa: University of Alabama Press.

Bucher, Rue, and Anselm Strauss. 1961. "Professions in Process." *American Journal of Sociology* 66: 325.

Butler, Judith. 1990. "Deconstruction and the Possibility of Justice: Comments on Bernasconi, Cornell, Miller, Weber." *Cardozo Law Review* 11: 1716.

Cahn, Edgar S., and Jean C. Cahn. 1964. "The War on Poverty: A Civilian Perspective." *Yale Law Journal* 73: 1317.

Cain, Patricia A. 2000. *Rainbow Rights: The Role of Lawyers and Courts in the Lesbian and Gay Civil Rights Movement*. Boulder, CO: Westview Press.

Carle, Susan. 2001. "Re-envisioning Models for Pro Bono Lawyering: Some Historical Reflections." *American University Journal of Gender and Social Policy* 9: 81.

———. 2002. "Race, Class, and Legal Ethics in the Early NAACP (1910–1920)" *Law and History Review* 20: 97.

Carlin, Jerome. 1962. *Lawyers on Their Own: A Study of Individual Practitioners in Chicago*. New Brunswick, NJ: Rutgers University Press.

Carter, Terry. 2001. "The In Crowd: Conservatives Who Sought Refuge in the Federalist Society Gain Clout." *ABA Journal* (September): 51.

Casper, Jonathan D. 1972. *Lawyers Before the Warren Court: Civil Liberties and Civil Rights, 1957–66*. Urbana: University of Illinois Press.

Chambers, David. n.d. Handout for Law and Society Association Panel (untitled).

Chase-Dunn, Christopher. 1991. *Globalization: Structures of the World Economy*. Cambridge, UK: Polity Press.

Cohen, Stanley. 1987. *Visions of Social Control*. Cambridge, UK: Polity Press.

Collier, Jane. 2001. "Durkheim Revisited: Human Rights as the Moral Discourse for the Post-Colonial, Post-Cold-War World." In *Human Rights: Concepts, Contests, Contingencies*, ed. Austin Sarat and Thomas R. Kearns. Ann Arbor: University of Michigan Press.

Cornell, Drucilla. 1988. "Post-Structuralism, the Ethical Relation, and the Law." *Cardozo Law Review* 9: 1587.

———. 1990. "From the Lighthouse: The Promise of Redemption and the Possibility of Legal Interpretation." *Cardozo Law Review* 11: 1697.

Coutin, Susan. 2001. "Cause Lawyering in the Shadow of the State: A U.S. Immigration Example." In *Cause Lawyering and the State in a Global Era*, ed. Austin Sarat and Stuart Scheingold. New York: Oxford University Press.

Cover, Robert. 1983. "The Supreme Court, 1982 Term—Foreword: Nomos and Narrative." *Harvard Law Review* 97: 4.

———. 1986. "Violence and the Word." *Yale Law Journal* 95: 1601.

Cronin, Kieran. 1992. *Rights and Christian Ethics*. New York: Cambridge University Press.

Cummings, Scott L. 2004. "The Politics of Pro Bono." *UCLA Law Review* 51: 1.

Davis, Martha. 2001. "Our Better Half: A Public Interest Lawyer Reflects on Pro Bono Lawyering and Social Change Litigation." *American University Journal of Gender and Social Policy* 9: 119.

Den Dulk, Kevin R. n.d. "In Legal Culture, but Not of It: The Cause Lawyering of Evangelical Conservatives." Unpublished paper.

Dezalay, Yves, and Bryant Garth. 2002. *The Internationalization of Palace Wars: Lawyers, Economists, and the Contest to Transform Latin American States.* Chicago: University of Chicago Press.

Diamond, Larry. 1994. "Rethinking Civil Society: Towards Democratic Consolidation." *Journal of Democracy* 5 (July 4–17).

Donzelot, Jacques. 1979. *The Policing of Families.* New York: Pantheon Books.

Dotan, Yoav. 2001. "The Global Language of Human Rights: Patterns of Cooperation Between State and Civil Rights Lawyers in Israel." In *Cause Lawyering and the State in a Global Era,* ed. Austin Sarat and Stuart Scheingold. New York: Oxford University Press.

Downs, Donald. 1985. *Nazis in Skokie: Freedom, Community, and the First Amendment.* Notre Dame, IN: Notre Dame University Press.

Epp, Charles R. 1998. *The Rights Revolution: Lawyers, Activists, and Supreme Courts in Comparative Perspective.* Chicago: University of Chicago Press.

Epstein, Cynthia Fuchs. 2002. "Stricture and Structure: The Social and Cultural Context of Pro Bono Work in Wall Street Firms." *Fordham Law Review* 70: 1689.

Epstein, Lee. 1985. *Conservatives in Court.* Knoxville: University of Tennessee Press.

Erlanger, Howard, and Douglas Klegon. 1978. "Socialization Effects of Professional School: The Law School Experience and Student Orientations to Public Interest Concerns." *Law and Society Review* 13: 11

Erlanger, Howard, Charles Epp, Mia Cahill, and Kathleen Grimes. 1996. "Law Student Idealism and Job Choice: Some New Data on an Old Question." *Law and Society Review* 30: 851.

Feinberg, Joel. 1998. *Rights, Justice, and the Bounds of Liberty: Essays in Social Philosophy.* Princeton, NJ: Princeton University Press.

Feldman, Marc. 1985. "Political Lessons: Legal Services for the Poor." *Georgetown Law Journal* 83: 1529.

Fine, Robert, and Sol Picciotto. 1992. "On Marxist Critiques of Law." In *The Critical Lawyers' Handbook,* ed. Ian Grigg-Spall and Paddy Ireland. London: Pluto Press.

Flathman, Richard. 1966. *The Public Interest: An Essay Concerning the Normative Discourse of Politics.* New York: John Wiley.

Fortney, Susan. 2003. "I Don't Have Time to Be Ethical: Addressing the Effects of Billable Hour Pressure." *Idaho Law Review* 39: 305.

Foster, James. 1981. "The 'Cooling Out' of Law Students: Facilitating Market Cooptation of Future Lawyers." *Law and Policy Quarterly* 3: 243

———. 1985. "Legal Education and the Production of Lawyers to (Re)Produce Liberal Capitalism." *Legal Studies Forum* 9: 179.

Freedman, Monroe. 1975. *Lawyers' Ethics in an Adversary System*. Indianapolis: Bobbs-Merrill.

Fried, Charles. 1976. "The Lawyer as Friend: The Moral Foundations of the Lawyer-Client Relation." *Yale Law Journal* 85: 1060.

Friedson, Elliot. 1972. *The Profession of Medicine*. New York: Dodd, Mead.

Gabel, Peter. 1982. "Reification and Legal Reasoning." In *Marxism and the Law*, ed. Piers Beirne and Richard Quinney. New York: John Wiley.

Garland, David. 1996. "The Limits of the Sovereign State: Strategies of Crime Control in Contemporary Society." *British Journal of Criminology* 36: 445.

Ginger, Ann Fagan, and Eugene M. Tobin, eds. 1988. *The National Lawyers Guild: From Roosevelt Through Reagan*. Philadelphia: Temple University Press.

Glendon, Mary Ann. 1994. *A Nation Under Lawyers: How the Crisis in the Legal Profession Is Transforming American Society*. New York: Farrar, Straus and Giroux.

Goode, William. 1957. "Community Within Community: The Professions," *American Sociological Review* 22: 194.

Goodrich, Chris. 1991. *Anarchy and Elegance: Confessions of a Journalist at Yale Law School*. Boston: Little, Brown.

Gordon, Robert. 1983. "Legal Thought and Legal Practice in the Age of the American Enterprise, 1870–1920." In *Professions and Professional Ideologies in America*, ed. G. Geison. Chapel Hill: University of North Carolina Press.

———. 1984. "The Ideal and the Actual." In *The New High Priests: Lawyers in Post–Civil War America*, ed. G. Gawalt. Westport, CT: Greenwood Press.

———. 1986. "Lawyers as the American Aristocracy." Unpublished essay.

———. 1988. "The Independence of Lawyers." *Boston University Law Review* 68: 1.

———. 1990. "Corporate Practice as a Public Calling." *Maryland Law Review* 49: 255.

Granfield, Robert. 1992. *Making Elite Lawyers: Visions of Law at Harvard and Beyond*. New York: Routledge.

Granfield, Robert, and Thomas Koenig. 1992a. "Pathways into Elite Law Firms: Professional Stratification and Social Networks." *Research in Policy and Society* 4: 503.

———. 1992b. "The Fate of Elite Idealism: Accommodation and Ideological Work at Harvard Law School." *Social Problems* 39: 315.

———. 2003. "It's Hard to Be a Human Being and a Lawyer: Young Attorneys' Confrontation with Ethical Ambiguity in Legal Practice." *West Virginia Law Review* 105: 495.

Greenberg, Jack. 1994. *Crusaders in the Courts: How a Dedicated Band of Lawyers Fought for the Civil Rights Revolution*. New York: Basic Books.

Grigg-Spall, Ian, and Paddy Ireland, eds. 1992. *The Critical Lawyers' Handbook*. London: Pluto Press.

Gross, Samuel. 1993. "The Romance of Revenge: Capital Punishment in America." *Studies in Law, Politics and Society* 13: 71.

Habermas, Jürgen. 1986. "The New Obscurity: The Crisis of the Welfare State and the Exhaustion of Utopian Energies." *Philosophy and Social Criticism* 11: 1.

Hagan, John, Marie Huxter, and Patricia Parker. 1988. "Class Structure and Legal Practice: Inequality and Mobility Among Toronto Lawyers." *Law and Society Review* 22: 9.

Hajjar, Lisa. 1997. "Cause Lawyering in Transnational Perspective: National Conflict and Human Rights in Israel / Palestine." *Law and Society Review* 31: 473.

———. 2001. "From the Fight for Legal Rights to the Promotion of Human Rights: Israel and Palestinian Cause Lawyers in the Trenches of Globalization." In *Cause Lawyering and the State in a Global Era*, ed. Austin Sarat and Stuart Scheingold. New York: Oxford University Press.

Halliday, Terence. 1987. *Beyond Monopoly: Lawyers, State Crises, and Professional Empowerment*. Chicago: University of Chicago Press.

———. 1998a. "Lawyers as Institution Builders: Constructing Markets, States, Civil Society, and Community." In *Crossing Boundaries: Traditions and Transformations in Law and Society Research*, ed. Austin Sarat, Marianne Constable, David Engel, Valerie Hans, and Susan Lawrence. Evanston, IL: Northwestern University Press.

———. 1998b. "Cause Lawyering and Transnational Networks: Pitfalls and Possibilities." Paper presented at the 1998 Law and Society Association Meeting.

Halliday, Terence, and Lucien Karpik, eds. 1997. *Lawyers and the Rise of Western Political Liberalism*. Oxford: Oxford University Press.

Haltom, William, and Michael McCann. Forthcoming. *Law's Lore: Tort Reform, Mass Media, and the Production of Legal Knowledge*. Chicago: University of Chicago Press.

Handler, Joel F., Ellen Jane Hollingsworth, and Howard Erlanger. 1978. *Lawyers and the Pursuit of Legal Rights*. New York: Academic Press.

Hans, Valerie P. 2000. *Business on Trial: The Civil Jury and Corporate Responsibility*. New Haven, CT: Yale University Press.

Hatcher, Laura J. Forthcoming. "Economic Libertarians, Property and Institutions: Linking Activism, Ideas and Identities Among Property Rights Advocates." In *The Worlds Cause Lawyers Make: Structure and Agency in Le-*

gal Practice, ed. Austin Sarat and Stuart A. Scheingold. Stanford, CA: Stanford University Press.

Heinz, Jack, and Edward Laumann. 1982. *Chicago Lawyers: The Social Structure of the Bar*. New York: Russell Sage Foundation

Heinz, John P., Anthony Paik, and Ann Southworth. 2003. "Lawyers for Conservative Causes: Clients, Ideology, and Social Distance." *Law and Society Review* 37: 5.

Held, David. 1995. *Democracy and the Global Order: From Modern State to Cosmopolitan Governance*. Cambridge, UK: Polity Press.

Hicks, Alexander M. 1999. *Social Democracy and Welfare Capitalism: A Century of Income Security Politics*. Ithaca, NY: Cornell University Press.

Hunter, James Davison. 1991. *Culture Wars: The Struggle to Define America*. New York: Basic Books.

Huntington, Samuel P. 1991. *The Third Wave: Democratization in the Late Twentieth Century*. Norman: University of Oklahoma Press.

Illich, Ivan. 1977. *Disabling Professions*. London: Marion Boyers.

Jameson, Fredric. 1998. "Notes on Globalization as a Philosophical Issue." In *The Cultures of Globalization*. Durham, NC: Duke University Press.

Johnson, Terrence. 1972. *Professions and Power*. London: Macmillan.

Kagan, Robert, and Robert Rosen. 1985. "On the Social Significance of Large Law Firm Practice." *Stanford Law Review* 37: 399.

Kahlenberg, Richard. 1992. *Broken Contract: A Memoir of Harvard Law School*. New York: Hill and Wang.

Kalman, Laura. 1996. *The Strange Career of Liberal Legalism*. New Haven, CT: Yale University Press.

Katz, Jack. 1982. *Poor People's Lawyers in Transition*. New Brunswick, NJ: Rutgers University Press.

Kelly, Michael J. 1994. *Lives of Lawyers: Journeys in the Organization of Practice*. Ann Arbor: University of Michigan Press.

Kennedy, Duncan. 1982. "Legal Education as Training in Hierarchy." In *The Politics of Law: A Progressive Critique*, ed. David Kairys. New York: Pantheon.

Kidder, Robert, and Setsuo Miyazawa. 1993. "Long-Term Strategies in Japanese Environmental Litigation." *Law and Social Inquiry* 18: 605.

Kilwein, John. 1998. "Still Trying: Cause Lawyering for the Poor and Disadvantaged in Pittsburgh, Pennsylvania." In *Cause Lawyering: Political Commitments and Professional Responsibilities*, ed. Austin Sarat and Stuart Scheingold. New York: Oxford University Press.

Kinoy, Arthur. 1983. *Rights on Trial: The Odyssey of a People's Lawyer*. Cambridge, MA: Harvard University Press.

Kluger, Richard. 1977. *Simple Justice: The History of Brown v. Board of Educa-*

tion and Black America's Struggle for Equal Justice. New York: Vintage Books.

Kramer, Daniel C. 1972. *Participatory Democracy: Developing Ideals of the Political Left.* Cambridge, MA: Schenkman Publishing.

Krishnan, Jayanth. Forthcoming. "Transgressive Cause Lawyering in the Developing World: The Case of India." In *The Worlds Cause Lawyers Make: Structure and Agency in Legal Practice,* ed. Austin Sarat and Stuart A. Scheingold. Stanford, CA: Stanford University Press.

Kronman, Anthony T. 1993. *The Lost Lawyer: Failing Ideals of the Legal Profession.* Cambridge, MA: Harvard University Press, Belknap Press.

Kubey, Craig. 1976. "Three Years of Adjustment: Where Your Ideals Go." *Juris Doctor* 6: 34.

Lacayo, Richard. 1992. "You Don't Always Get Perry Mason," *Time,* June 1, p. 38.

Landon, Donald. 1990. *Country Lawyers: The Impact of Context on Professional Practice.* New York: Praeger.

Lardent, Esther. 1999. "Positional Conflicts in the Pro Bono Context." *Fordham Law Review* 67: 2279.

Larson, Magali Sarfatti. 1977. *The Rise of Professionalism.* Berkeley: University of California Press.

Lasswell, Harold. 1962. "The Public Interest: Proposing Principles of Content and Procedure." In *The Public Interest,* ed. Carl Friedrich. New York: Atherton Press.

Lempert, Richard, David Chambers, and Terry Adams. 2000. "Michigan's Minority Graduates in Practice: The River Runs Through Law School." *Law and Social Inquiry* 25: 395.

Lev, Daniel. 1998. "Lawyers' Causes in Indonesia and Malaysia." In *Cause Lawyering: Political Commitments and Professional Responsibilities,* ed. Austin Sarat and Stuart Scheingold. New York: Oxford University Press.

Levine, Andrew. 1981. *Liberal Democracy: A Critique of Its Theory.* New York: Columbia University Press.

Liebman, Robert C., and Robert Wuthnow. 1983. *The New Christian Right.* New York: Aldine.

Litvin, Daniel B. 2003. *Empires of Profit: Commerce, Conquest, and Corporate Responsibility.* New York: Texere.

Llewellyn, Karl. 1960. *The Bramble Bush: On Our Law and Its Study.* Dobbs Ferry, NY: Oceana.

Long, Norton. 1952. "Bureaucracy and Constitutionalism," *American Political Science Review* 12: 808.

López, Gerald P. 1992. *Rebellious Lawyering: One Chicano's Vision of Progressive Law Practice.* Boulder, CO: Westview Press.

Lorde, Audre. 1984. "The Master's Tools Will Never Dismantle the Master's House." In *Sister Outsider*. Trumansburg, NY: Crossing Press.

Lowi, Theodore J. 1979. *The End of Liberalism: The Second Republic of the United States*. New York: Norton.

Luban, David. 1984. "The Adversary System Excuse." In *The Good Lawyer: Lawyers' Roles and Lawyers' Ethics*, ed. David Luban. Totowa, NJ: Rowman and Allenheld.

————. 1988. *Lawyers and Justice: An Ethical Study*. Princeton, NJ: Princeton University Press.

————. 2003. "Taking Out the Adversary: The Assault on Progressive Public-Interest Lawyers." *California Law Review* 91: 209.

MacEwan, Arthur. 1999. *Neo-Liberalism or Democracy? Economic Strategy, Markets, and Alternatives for the 21st Century*. New York: Zed Books.

Machan, Tibor R. 1974. *The Libertarian Alternative: Essays in Social and Political Philosophy*. Chicago: Nelson-Hall.

Maute, Judith. 2002. "Changing Conceptions of Pro Bono Responsibilities: From Chance Noblesse Oblige to Stated Expectations." *Tulane Law Review* 77: 91.

McCann, Michael. 1994. *Rights at Work: Pay Equity Reform and the Politics of Legal Mobilization*. Chicago: University of Chicago Press.

McCann, Michael, and Helena Silverstein. 1998. "Rethinking Law's Allurements: A Relational Analysis of Social Movement Lawyers in the United States." In *Cause Lawyering: Political Commitments and Professional Responsibilities*, ed. Austin Sarat and Stuart Scheingold. New York: Oxford University Press.

Meilli, Stephen. 2001. "Latin American Cause-Lawyering Networks." In *Cause Lawyering and the State in a Global Era*, ed. Austin Sarat and Stuart Scheingold. New York: Oxford University Press.

Menkel-Meadow, Carrie J. 1992. "Is Altruism Possible in Lawyering?" *Georgia State University Law Review* 8: 385.

————. 1998. "The Causes of Cause Lawyering: Toward an Understanding of the Motivation and Commitment of Social Justice Lawyers." In *Cause Lawyering: Political Commitments and Professional Responsibilities*, ed. Austin Sarat and Stuart Scheingold. New York: Oxford University Press.

Merry, Sally Engle. 1995. "Wife Battering and the Ambiguities of Rights." In *Identities, Politics, and Rights*, ed. Austin Sarat and Thomas R. Kearns. Ann Arbor: University of Michigan Press.

Miller, Mark C. 1995. *The High Priests of American Politics: The Role of Lawyers in American Political Institutions*. Knoxville: University of Tennessee Press.

Miyazawa, Setsuo. 1996. "Cause Lawyering by a Cartelized Legal Profession: Profiles in Cause Lawyering in Japan." Unpublished paper.

Mnookin, Robert, and Lewis Kornhauser. 1979. "Bargaining in the Shadow of the Law." *Yale Law Journal* 85: 950.

Morag-Levine, Noga. 2001. "The Politics of Imported Rights: Transplantation and Transformation in an Israeli Environmental Cause-Lawyering Organization." In *Cause Lawyering and the State in a Global Era*, ed. Austin Sarat and Stuart Scheingold. New York: Oxford University Press.

Morgan, Richard E. 1984. *Disabling America: The "Rights Industry" in Our Time*. New York: Basic Books.

Nelson, Robert, and David Trubek. 1992a. "Introduction: New Problems and New Paradigms in Studies of the Legal Profession." In *Lawyers' Ideals/Lawyers' Practices: Transformations in the American Legal Profession*, ed. Robert Nelson, David Trubek, and Rayman Solomon. Ithaca, NY: Cornell University Press.

———. 1992b. "Arenas of Professionalism: The Professional Ideologies of Lawyers in Context." In *Lawyers' Ideals/Lawyers' Practices: Transformations in the American Legal Profession*, ed. Robert Nelson, David Trubek, and Rayman Solomon. Ithaca, NY: Cornell University Press.

Niemeyer, Gerhart. 1962. "Public Interest and Private Utility." In *The Public Interest*, ed. Carl Friedrich. New York: Atherton Press.

Noll, Mark A. 2001. *American Evangelical Christianity: An Introduction*. Oxford: Blackwell Publishers.

Noonan, John. 1976. *Persons and Masks of the Law: Cardozo, Holmes, Jefferson, Wythe as Makers of the Masks*. New York: Farrar, Straus and Giroux.

Norris, Donald, and Lyke Thompson, eds. 1995. *The Politics of Welfare Reform*. Thousand Oaks, CA: Sage Publications.

O'Brien, Sean. 1990. "A Step Toward Fairness in Capital Litigation: Missouri Resource Center." *William Mitchell Law Review* 16: 633.

Offe, Claus. 1984. *Contradictions of the Welfare State*. Cambridge, MA: MIT Press.

Parekh, Bhikhu. 1993. "The Cultural Particularity of Liberal Democracy." In *Prospects for Democracy*, ed. David Held. Stanford, CA: Stanford University Press.

Parsons, Talcott. 1962. "The Law and Social Control." In *Law and Sociology: Exploratory Essays*, ed. William M. Evan. New York: Free Press of Glencoe.

Peller, Gary. 1985. "The Metaphysics of American Law." *California Law Review* 73: 1151.

Pennock, J. Roland, and John W. Chapman, eds. 1983. *Liberal Democracy*. New York: New York University Press.

Piven, Frances Fox, and Richard Cloward. 1972. *Regulating the Poor: The Functions of Public Welfare*. New York: Vintage.

Putnam, Robert. 1995. "Bowling Alone." *Journal of Democracy* 6: 65.

———. 1996. "The Strange Disappearance of Civic America." *The American Prospect* 24: 34.

Rabinowitz, Victor. 1996. *Unrepentant Leftist: A Lawyer's Memoir.* Urbana: University of Illinois Press.

Rabinowitz, Victor, and Tim Ledwith, eds. 1987. *A History of the National Lawyers Guild.* New York: National Lawyers Guild.

Reisman, David A. 1999. *Conservative Capitalism: The Social Economy.* New York: St. Martin's Press.

Rhode, Deborah. 1999. "Cultures of Commitment: Pro Bono for Lawyers and Law Students." *Fordham Law Review* 67: 2415.

———. 2000a. "Cultures of Commitment: Pro Bono for Lawyers and Law Students." In *Ethics in Practice: Lawyers' Roles, Responsibilities, and Regulation,* ed. Deborah Rhode. New York; Oxford University Press.

———. 2000b. *In the Interests of Justice: Reforming the Legal Profession.* New York: Oxford University Press.

Richmond, Douglas. 2002. "The New Law Firm Economy, Billable Hours, and Professional Responsibility." *Hofstra Law Review* 29: 207.

Rose, Nikolas. 1996a. "The Death of the Social? Re-Figuring the Territory of Government." *Economy and Society* 25: 327.

———. 1996b. "Expertise and the Government of Conduct." *Studies in Law, Politics, and Society* 14: 359.

———. 1999. *Powers of Freedom: Reframing Political Thought.* Cambridge: Cambridge University Press

Rosen, Robert Eli. 2001. "On the Social Significance of Critical Lawyering." *Legal Ethics* 3: 169.

Rueschemeyer, Dietrich, Evelyne Huber Stephens, and John D. Stephens. 1992. *Capitalist Development and Democracy.* Chicago: University of Chicago Press.

Rush, Norman. 1994. "What Was Socialism and Why We Will All Miss It So Much." *The Nation* 268: 90.

Ruthenbeck, Arthur. 1989. "Dueling with Death in Federal Courts." *Criminal Justice* 3: 3.

Santos, Boaventura de Sousa. 1995. *Toward a New Common Sense: Law, Science, and Politics in the Paradigmatic Transition.* New York: Routledge.

Sarat, Austin. 1993. "Law's Two Lives: Humanist Visions and Professional Education." *Yale Journal of Law and the Humanities* 5: 201.

———. 1998a. "Between (the Presence of) Violence and (the Possibility of) Justice: Lawyering Against Capital Punishment." In *Cause Lawyering: Political Commitments and Professional Responsibilities,* ed. Austin Sarat and Stuart Scheingold. New York: Oxford University Press.

———. 1998b. "Recapturing the Spirit of *Furman*: The American Bar Association and the New Abolitionist Politics." *Law and Contemporary Problems* 61: 5.

———. 2001. "State Transformation and the Struggle for Symbolic Capital: Cause Lawyers, the Organized Bar, and Capital Punishment in the United States." In *Cause Lawyering and the State in a Global Era*, ed. Austin Sarat and Stuart Scheingold. New York: Oxford University Press.

Sarat, Austin, and Thomas R. Kearns. 2001. "The Unsettled Status of Human Rights: An Introduction." In *Human Rights: Concepts, Contests, Contingencies*, ed. Austin Sarat and Thomas R. Kearns. Ann Arbor: University of Michigan Press.

Sarat, Austin, and Stuart Scheingold. 1998a. *Cause Lawyering: Political Commitments and Professional Responsibilities*. New York: Oxford University Press.

———. 1998b. "Cause Lawyering and the Reproduction of Professional Authority: An Introduction." In *Cause Lawyering: Political Commitments and Professional Responsibilities*, ed. Austin Sarat and Stuart Scheingold. New York: Oxford University Press.

———, eds. 2001a. *Cause Lawyering and the State in a Global Era*. New York: Oxford University Press.

———. 2001b. "State Transformation, Globalization, and the Possibilities of Cause Lawyering: An Introduction." In *Cause Lawyering and the State in a Global Era*, ed. Austin Sarat and Stuart Scheingold. New York: Oxford University Press.

———. Forthcoming. *The Worlds Cause Lawyers Make: Structure and Agency in Legal Practice*. Stanford, CA: Stanford University Press.

Scheingold, Stuart A. 1974. *The Politics of Rights: Lawyers, Public Policy, and Political Change*. New Haven, CT: Yale University Press.

———. 1998. "The Struggle to Politicize Legal Practice: Left-Activist Lawyering in Seattle." In *Cause Lawyering: Political Commitments and Professional Responsibilities*, ed. Austin Sarat and Stuart Scheingold. New York: Oxford University Press.

———. 2001. "Cause Lawyering and Democracy in Transnational Perspective: A Postscript." In *Cause Lawyering and the State in a Global Era*, ed. Austin Sarat and Stuart Scheingold. New York: Oxford University Press.

Scheingold, Stuart A., and Anne Bloom. 1998. "Transgressive Cause Lawyering: Practice Sites and the Politicization of the Professional." *International Journal of the Legal Profession* 5: 209.

Schneyer, Theodore. 2002. "Reforming Law Practice in the Pursuit of Justice: The Perils of Privileging 'Public' over Professional Values." *Fordham Law Review* 70: 1831.

Schubert, Glendon. 1960. *The Public Interest: A Critique of the Theory of a Political Concept.* Glencoe, IL: The Free Press.

Shamir, Ronen. 1995. *Managing Legal Uncertainty: Elite Lawyers in the New Deal.* Durham, NC: Duke University Press.

———. 1998. "De-centering of State and Cause." Paper presented at the 1998 Law and Society Association Meeting.

———. Forthcoming. "South Africa and the Pharmaceutical Industries: A Test for Corporate Social Responsibility?" In *The Worlds Cause Lawyers Make: Structure and Agency in Legal Practice,* ed. Austin Sarat and Stuart A. Scheingold. Stanford, CA: Stanford University Press.

Shamir, Ronen, and Sara Chinsky. 1998. "Destruction of Houses and Construction of a Cause: Lawyers and Bedouins in Israeli Courts." In *Cause Lawyering: Political Commitments and Professional Responsibilities,* ed. Austin Sarat and Stuart Scheingold. New York: Oxford University Press.

Shamir, Ronen, and Neta Ziv. 2001. "State-Oriented Community Lawyering for a Cause: A Tale of Two Strategies." In *Cause Lawyering and the State in a Global Era,* ed. Austin Sarat and Stuart Scheingold. New York: Oxford University Press.

Shapiro, Susan. 2003. "Bushwhacking the Ethical High Road: Conflicts of Interest in the Practice of Law and Real Life." *Law and Social Inquiry* 28: 87.

Silver, Charles, and Frank B. Cross. 2000. "What's Not to Like About Being a Lawyer? Lawyer: A Life of Counsel and Controversy." *Yale Law Journal* 109: 1443.

Silverstein, Helena. 1996. *Unleashing Rights: Law, Meaning, and the Animal Rights Movement.* Ann Arbor: University of Michigan Press.

Simon, Jonathan. 1997. "Governing Through Crime." *The Crime Conundrum: Essays in Criminal Justice,* ed. Lawrence M. Friedman and George Fisher. Boulder, CO: Westview Press.

Simon, William. 1978. "The Ideology of Advocacy." *Wisconsin Law Review* 1978: 30.

———. 1984. "Visions of Practice in Legal Thought." *Stanford Law Review* 36: 469.

———. 1998. *The Practice of Justice: A Theory of Lawyers' Ethics.* Cambridge, MA: Harvard University Press.

Solomon, Rayman. 1992. "Five Crises or One: The Concept of Legal Professionalism, 1925–1960." In *Lawyers' Ideals/Lawyers' Practices: Transformations in the American Legal Profession,* ed. Robert Nelson, David Trubek, and Rayman Solomon. Ithaca, NY: Cornell University Press.

Soper, J. Christopher. 1994. *Evangelical Christianity in the United States and*

Great Britain: Religious Beliefs, Political Choices. New York: New York University Press.

Southworth, Ann. Forthcoming. "Professional Identity and Political Commitment Among Lawyers for Conservative Causes." In *The Worlds Cause Lawyers Make: Structure and Agency in Legal Practice*, ed. Austin Sarat and Stuart A. Scheingold. Stanford, CA: Stanford University Press.

Spaulding, Norman. 2003. "Reinterpreting Professional Identity." *University of Colorado Law Review* 74: 1.

St. James, Warren D. 1958. *The National Association for the Advancement of Colored People: A Case Study in Pressure Groups.* New York: Exposition Press.

Sterett, Susan. 1998. "Caring About Individual Cases: Immigration Lawyering in Britain." In *Cause Lawyering: Political Commitments and Professional Responsibilities*, ed. Austin Sarat and Stuart Scheingold. New York: Oxford University Press.

Stevens, Robert. 1983. *Law School: Legal Education in America from the 1850s to the 1980s.* Chapel Hill: University of North Carolina Press.

Stover, Robert. 1989. *Making It and Breaking It: The Fate of Public Interest Commitment During Law School.* Urbana: University of Illinois Press

Teles, Steven. 2003. "The Politics of Legal Counter-Mobilization: The Birth and Evolution of the Federalist Society." Unpublished manuscript.

Teson, Fernando. 1985. "International Human Rights and Cultural Relativism." *Virginia Journal of International Law* 25: 869.

Thody, Philip. 1995. *The Conservative Imagination.* New York: Pinter Publishers.

Thomson, Alan. 1992. "Foreword—Critical Approaches to Law: Who Needs Legal Theory?" In *The Critical Lawyers' Handbook*, ed. Ian Grigg-Spall and Paddy Ireland. London: Pluto Press.

Thompson, Judith Jarvis. 1990. *The Realm of Rights.* Cambridge, MA: Harvard University Press.

Tocqueville, Alexis de. 1876. *Democracy in America*, vol. 1. Trans. Henry Reeve. Boston: John Allyn.

Tonry, Michael. 1995. *Malign Neglect—Race, Crime, and Punishment in America.* New York: Oxford University Press.

Trembath, Kern. 1987. *Evangelical Theories of Biblical Inspiration: A Review and Proposal.* New York: Oxford University Press.

Trubek, Louise, and M. Elizabeth Kransberger. 1998. "Critical Lawyers: Social Justice and the Structures of Private Practice." In *Cause Lawyering: Political Commitments and Professional Responsibilities*, ed. Austin Sarat and Stuart Scheingold. New York: Oxford University Press.

Truman, David. 1951. *The Governmental Process.* New York: Knopf.

Turow, Scott. 1977. *One L.* New York: Penguin Books.

Unger, Roberto. 1976. *Law in Modern Society.* New York: The Free Press.

Walker, Samuel. 1992. *The American Civil Liberties Union: An Annotated Bibliography.* New York: Garland Publishing.

Weissbrodt, David. 1989. "Human Rights: An Historical Perspective." In *Human Rights*, ed. Peter Davies. London: Routledge.

Wernz, William. 2002. "The Ethics of Large Law Firms—Responses and Reflections." *Georgetown Journal of Legal Ethics* 16: 175.

White, Lucie. 2001. "Two Worlds of Ghanaian Cause Lawyers." In *Cause Lawyering and the State in a Global Era*, ed. Austin Sarat and Stuart Scheingold, 35. New York: Oxford University Press.

Wilkens, Robert. 1987. "The Person You're Supposed to Become: The Politics of the Law School Experience." *University of Toronto Faculty Law Review* 45: 98.

Wilson, Richard. 1996. "Human Rights, Culture and Context: An Introduction." In *Human Rights, Culture and Context*, ed. Richard Wilson. London: Pluto Press.

Wizner, Stephen. 2001. "Beyond Skills Training." *Clinical Law Review* 7: 327.

———. 2002. "The Law School Clinic: Legal Education in the Interests of Justice." *Fordham Law Review* 70: 1929.

Woods, Patricia. Forthcoming. "Cause Lawyers and the Judicial Community in Israel: Legal Change in a Diffuse Normative Community." In *The Worlds Cause Lawyers Make: Structure and Agency in Legal Practice*, ed. Austin Sarat and Stuart A. Scheingold. Stanford, CA: Stanford University Press.

Young, Alison, and Austin Sarat. 1994. "Introduction to 'Beyond Criticism: Law, Power and Ethics.'" *Social and Legal Studies: An International Journal* 3: 323.

Index

Abel, Richard, 132, 144n2
abortion-related cause lawyering,
50, 110; compensation, 80; conflict-of-interest issues, 79; evangelical, 80, 114, 115, 116, 117,
149n8; practice site, 96
accommodations: pro bono work in
corporate firms, 78–80; salaried
practice in public and private
agencies, 85–88; small firm, 93–95
accountability, liberal democracy,
102, 108
accreditation standards, 26
Acheson, Dean, 14
Administrative Office of the Courts,
45
advertising, prohibited, 33
advocacy, ideology of, 8, 10, 26, 73,
80, 86
affordability: and social justice, 15–
16. See also legal services programs; poor
Africa: cause lawyering, 131, 132;
transnational networks, 139
African-Americans: ABA excluding,
33; NAACP, 4, 40, 42, 81, 100–101;
school desegregation, 40–41, 42

alienation, lawyers', 1–2, 8, 23, 64,
73
altruism, 7, 54–55, 69, 73; mixed-
motive, 147n1
American Bar Association (ABA) /
organized bar, 24–29, 31; and
cause lawyering, 24–25, 29, 40,
43–50, 69–70, 127–28; Commission on Professionalism, 28; corporate alliance, 33, 34–35, 38; and
death penalty, 46–48, 121; disciplinary mechanisms, 26; ethics,
33, 75, 144n1, 145n5; legal education alliances, 33, 34, 35; and legal
services programs, 41, 44–45, 49;
vs. non-WASP influx, 32–34; and
pro bono work, 75; social injustice
associated with, 41. See also legal
professionalism
American Center for Law and Justice (ACLJ), 116
American Civil Liberties Union
(ACLU), 16, 40, 68, 100–101, 110,
149n6
anti-ism, 121–22, 150–51n15
anxiety, lawyers', 1–2, 23
appellate work, 16, 83